D0624786

WEiRD SCiENCE
MAD MARVELS
from the Way-Out World

by Matt Lake and Randy Fairbanks

STERLING CHILDREN'S BOOKS
New York

To the weird British scientists Joseph Priestley and Alexander Fleming. The first invented soda and called oxygen "dephlogisticated air." The other painted pictures with bacteria. Really ... what's not to love about men who would do things like that? –Matt Lake

To Lance and Mallory, and to my father, who helps them with their science homework. –Randy Fairbanks

STERLING CHILDREN'S BOOKS
New York

An Imprint of Sterling Publishing
387 Park Avenue South
New York, NY 10016

ISBN 978-1-4027-6041-9

Photography and illustration credits are found on page 118 and constitute an extension of this copyright page.

Distributed in Canada by Sterling Publishing
C/o Canadian Manda Group, 165 Dufferin Street
Toronto, Ontario, Canada M6K 3H6
Distributed in the United Kingdom by GMC Distribution Services
Castle Place, 166 High Street, Lewes, East Sussex, England BN7 1XU
Distributed in Australia by Capricorn Link (Australia) Pty. Ltd.
P.O. Box 704, Windsor, NSW 2756, Australia

For information about custom editions, special sales, and premium and corporate purchases, please contact Sterling Special Sales
at 800-805-5489 or specialsales@sterlingpublishing.com.

Printed in China
Lot #:
10 9 8 7 6 5 4 3 2 1
04/12

www.sterlingpublishing.com/kids

CONTENTS

A SCIENTIFIC SURVEY OF FAR-OUT PHENOMENA!

Introduction

We'll never forget the first time we saw a scientist at work. We were both kids, and the scientist we were watching was the star of an old black-and-white movie. He wore a white lab coat and goggles, and he ran about the place yelling at the top of his voice as thunder rolled and lightning flashed. "It's alive!" he screamed, "ALIVE!"

Yes, our first brush with the joys of science was watching Dr. Frankenstein bringing his monster to life. We didn't know it at the time, but the story of *Frankenstein* was inspired by the work of a real-life scientist, Luigi Galvani, who, back in the 1700s, made the muscles of dead animals twitch by passing electricity through them. But as we watched this dramatic scene on our TV sets, the same thought ran through our heads: *Science is really cool!*

Before we go on, we should probably introduce ourselves. We are Matt Lake and Randy Fairbanks, and we are researchers and writers at Weird Central, which is a mysterious base in a secret location, where news of all the weird things in the world eventually ends up. The whole operation is run by two very strange characters—Mark Sceurman and Mark Moran—who are like two Dr. Frankensteins, but without the white lab coats and goggles. Oh, and there are no monsters here either, though we do hear about a lot of them.

Weird Central

What's Weird Central like? Imagine a science lab with strange chemicals bubbling through glass tubes and vast data banks of weirdness that whir and click with up-to-the-minute news of all the amazing things that ever happened. Imagine an office in the back of the lab where phones ring off their hooks and e-mails come in by the thousands. And imagine teams of researchers analyzing all these bits of data and producing elaborate reports on them.

Well, Weird Central is nothing like that. But we do collect strange stories and facts, and we've put the best and weirdest science-related ones in this book. In these pages, you will find some wild tales. Read closely and you'll learn the answers to these burning questions:

- Who invented the world of electronics but also thought he could make machines that could photograph thoughts and communicate with dead people?

- Which member of the animal kingdom hears through its knees?

- Which other member of the animal kingdom leaves behind poop that can be made into paper?

- Which four chemicals can be combined to make both air and chocolate?

If you can't answer these questions, you clearly need to read *Weird Science*! And if you already know the answers . . . we should talk.

The famous Boris Karloff as Frankenstein's monster in the famous 1931 movie *Frankenstein*. Weird science at its best!

Hello, this is Weird Central. How may I direct your call?

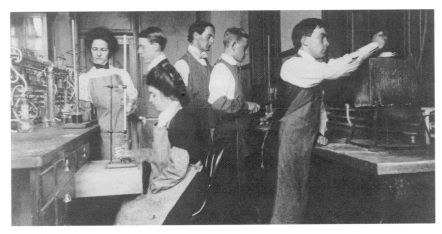

The staff at Weird Central either testing an important theory . . . or making lunch.

Turn the page . . . The weirdness awaits you!

It's alive! ALIVE!

ZANY ZOOLOGY

There's a whole branch of science dedicated to animals. It's called *zoology*, and the people who study it are called *zoologists*. They are the ones responsible for (what else?), ZOOS, where we can see and find out about all kinds of exotic creatures. And, boy, is our world full of weird and wonderful animals! In fact, there are more mysterious creatures out there than most of us can dream of.

For example, what would you think if someone told you there are real dragons that can lick you to death? Would you believe it? You should—there's a species of big lizards called Komodo dragons, with spit so full of bacteria that one drop of it on a scratch or cut is enough to give you a deadly infection that could kill you in days! Even creatures you think you know are weird. Did you know that a lobster's teeth are in its stomach? Or that the world's smallest frog could sit on your thumbnail? Or that the world's smallest monkey is no longer than your toothbrush? All true. So check your toothbrush for any stray monkeys, make sure your thumbs are free of frogs, and read on. The animal kingdom's a weird place, and you're going to need your wits about you.

How 'bout a little kiss?

Let's hope I never need braces!

Mad Masses of Mammals

Mammals are an amazing group of animals—and they're the group we belong to. Mammals have these things in common: they have warm blood, have hair, and give birth to live young, and the mothers produce milk to feed their young. After that, however, things begin to get very interesting (and weird). For instance, the mammal family includes the largest animal ever—the 200-ton, 108-foot-long blue whale. This animal is so big that its heart weighs as much as ten full-grown people. Meanwhile, at the other end of the scale is the world's smallest mammal, the bumblebee bat. It weighs about as much as four mini marshmallows. So without further ado, here's a glimpse of some marvelously weird mammals.

A blue whale going for a dive.

Some scientists claim that the Etruscan shrew is actually lighter than the bumblebee bat; however, it's a little longer, so the bat wins!

You best steer clear of a blue whale's mouth!

Ligers and Tiglons and What?!

Did you know tigers and lions could mate? It's not something they necessarily care to do; however, it does happen, especially in zoos. Ligers are a cross between a male lion and a female tiger. They are the largest cats in the world, and a male liger can stand up to one and a half feet taller than its lion dad. Ligers like to swim (just like tigers) and are sociable (just like lions). They can have stripes *and* manes. Ligers don't live in the wild, but you can visit them at the few zoos around the world that have them. By the way, don't confuse ligers with tiglons, which are a cross between (you guessed it!) a male tiger and a female lion.

Two ligers at an amusement park in South Korea.

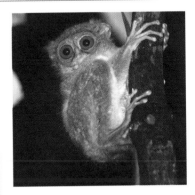

The Philippine tarsier is one of the smallest primates in the world. As you can see, it has the largest eye-to-body size ratio of all mammals, which is good, since tarsiers need those big eyes to hunt insects and small birds at night.

CHAPTER 1

Anybody Seen My Clothes?

So, what's so weird about East African naked mole rats? First of all, they don't feel pain in their skin. Next, they can't really regulate their body temperature like most mammals can. Then there's the fact that they can't see very well since they spend most of their life deep underground. Baby naked mole rats eat poop until they can digest solid food. Oh yeah, they have relatively little hair (for a mammal) and look like this!

Panda Poop Paper

Pandas, native to China, eat bamboo shoots. In fact, 99 percent of their diet consists of bamboo, which gives them plenty of fiber! This leads to one interesting but sort of gross fact: panda poop can be made into paper. Just be glad that it's not the paper you're holding right now!

Marsupial Madness

Marsupials are a type of mammal that gives birth to relatively undeveloped offspring. Nearly 70 percent of marsupials in the world are found in Australia and New Guinea, and probably the most famous marsupial of all is the kangaroo. Newborn kangaroos are about the same size as a paper clip. It's no surprise then that they crawl straight into their mama's pouch and stay there until they're big enough to hop around by themselves.

Meanwhile, the marsupial koala has humanlike fingerprints. No two koalas have the same print, so they can't go around committing koala crimes without fear of being caught by the koala cops.

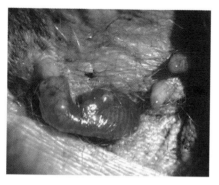

I want a lawyer.

A newborn kangaroo safe inside its mother's pouch.
Kinda creepy looking, eh?!

The Monotremes

If you think marsupials are weird mammals, just wait till you meet the monotremes. Ask anyone what makes a mammal a mammal and they'll tell you that they have hair and warm blood, and mammal moms give birth to live young and produce milk to feed them. Monotremes do all these things except for one: they lay eggs! No other mammals do this, and no other egg-laying creatures have fur and make milk. There are two members of the monotreme family, the platypus and the echidna or spiny anteater, and they both look really strange.

A platypus looks kind of like an otter, except that it has a big flat tail like a beaver's. And a big flat beak like a duck's. Oh, and on its hind legs it has a spike that gives off a nasty venom like a scorpion's.

The echidna looks like a giant mole. But it has a scattered coat of spines like a balding porcupine. And it has a tubelike beak that it uses to suck up a diet of ants.

The plural of "platypus" is not "platipi." It's just plain old "platypus."

I'm confused.

Echidnas are native to Australia and New Guinea. After mating, the female lays one soft-shelled egg and places it in her pouch. The egg hatches ten days later, and then the young echidna (known as a puggle) remains in the pouch for nearly two months.

Mammals in Armor

You probably don't think of the armadillo as particularly weird. It's a mammal with a leathery skin so thick that Spanish-speaking people called it "the little armored one." And you've probably seen enough pictures of armadillos that they look normal to you. Well, if that's what you think, go to Argentina and check out their native armored ones, the pink fairy armadillos. They look to us like someone took a white rabbit, gave it giant lizard feet, and glued pink armor on its back.

Yes, pink is his favorite color.

Just don't laugh at the pink fairy armadillo, because another Argentinean armadillo may stand up for its silly-looking cousin. The screaming hairy armadillo is a mean-looking beast with mad hair sticking up through its armor and a long wolverine-like jaw.

The screaming hairy armadillo in a rare quiet moment.

But there's another kind of armored mammal that makes even the pink fairy armadillo look normal. It lives in China, Thailand, and other East Asian countries; eats ants and other insects; and rolls into a ball to sleep during the day. It's called the pangolin, although jokers like to call it a walking artichoke or a pinecone with a tail. That's because the pangolin's body is covered with hundreds of what look like fish scales. These plates of keratin (that's the same stuff that makes human fingernails) act as both armor and weapon—they shield the pangolin from attack, and when it rolls up, they stick out a bit and can slice anything that rubs against them. And wait till you hear about its tongue! It slides back all the way into its chest, where it gets covered with sticky spit, and then it shoots out to catch ants and termites. A pangolin's tongue is almost half the length of its body—full-grown pangolins are about three feet long and their tongues can shoot sixteen inches from their mouths!

Cat got your tongue?

The pangolin's scales are made of the same stuff as your fingernails!

Enough with the mammals! How about some other critters?

Awesome Owls

Though not as all-seeing as dragonflies, owls can twist their heads almost all the way around. A complete circle is 360 degrees, and an owl can turn its head 280 degrees in either direction. (Dragonflies have an almost 360-degree view!) With a couple of twists of its head, an owl can scope out the world all around it without moving a muscle below its neck. It needs this ability for one simple reason: it can't move its eyeballs.

This Eurasian eagle owl has its head screwed on right.

Freaky Fish

The crab in the Disney movie *The Little Mermaid* had it right: "it's better down where it's wetter"—at least, it is if you're looking for weird animals. Under the sea is one of the best refuges for strange life. They live in a deep, dark world teeming with vicious predators and extremes of cold and hot that could kill a human in moments. And they have strange-looking bodies that help them survive in that hostile environment. Don't believe us? Take a look!

One look at this guy should be enough to prove our point. Known as Shaefer's anglerfish, only three have ever been seen. "Fishing poles" on its head attract prey, which swim just above its huge mouth. Then, it sucks 'em in. This specimen was named "Bubba" by the scientists who found it. It was returned to its home after a quick examination.

Is It a Fish or a Submarine?

Two thousand feet deep in the Pacific Ocean there's a fish that science has known about for a hundred years, but we've only just found a live one. Why has it been so hard to find? Because it has the strangest eyes we've ever heard of. They're barrel-shaped, like binoculars, and point upward, so they can always see predators, food . . . and fishing nets! To protect these eyes from damage, this fish doesn't have eyelids like we do, but instead has a see-through head with its eyes set right in the middle of it.

The barreleye fish's domed, transparent head lets in more light to see with— which is useful because it's very dark that deep in the ocean. It also gives a wide viewing window so the eyes can swivel around and see the world in front of it and to the sides. This makes it hard for anything to sneak up on the fish, so science has only studied live ones for a few decades. Until then, the only samples ever seen were dead ones that must have been looking elsewhere when they were caught in fishing nets.

Underwater Lightbulb

The glass squid spends most of its time trying to be invisible. Its body is transparent, and the only part of it you can see in normal light (that is, in midwater ocean depths) is a little red organ in the middle of its body that's a bit like the squid's liver. Unlike humans, the squid can twist its liver around a bit to make sure that only the thin side faces any predators, so that it'll either be hidden or look too small to bother eating. Actually, even if a predator took a bite of glass squid, it wouldn't enjoy it very much:

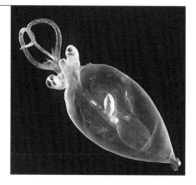

Glass squid range in size from 3 inches to nearly 10 feet in length.

the squid uses a bladder filled with ammonia solution to help it float or go deeper into the ocean. Ammonia is a strong chemical — a mouthful is enough to put off any hungry fish!

There are about sixty species of glass squid, and some of them are also bioluminescent, which means they generate their own light. Imagine that . . . a transparent animal that gives off light—a living lightbulb! They also have an organ behind their eyes that acts like the bill of a baseball cap—it stops the light they generate from dazzling them.

The Weirdest Animal Alive

We have a candidate for the coveted title of "The Weirdest Animal Alive," and we want your vote! The creature we are thinking of lives on the bed of the Pacific Ocean. It breathes toxic gases, but it has no lungs. It digests poisons, but it has no stomach. It survives in very hot water near underwater volcanoes, but it doesn't get cooked. And half of its body weight is made of bacteria, but it's not infected.

This creature is called a giant tube worm, and it's the most unusual creature in the world. You may have heard in earth science classes that all our food comes from the sun. Plants use sun energy to turn carbon dioxide from the air into food for plants, and everything else on Earth uses the plants for food. That's basically how our food web works. The tube worm is the exception.

Giant tube worms can live up to several miles deep on the ocean floor.

As you can guess from its name, the giant tube worm is a big tube planted in the seabed, with its bright red mouth floating around with the current. Think of an overcooked piece of macaroni that's several inches wide and up to seven feet long—that's what a giant tube worm is like. Down where it lives is too deep for the sun to feed plants. Very few other animals even swim down there. And unlike other deep-water creatures, the tube worm doesn't scavenge dead things that sink down to their level. So what is there to eat? The only thing to sustain life down there is toxic volcanic gas that bubbles through cracks in the seabed.

Volcanoes give off lava and a lot of heat, but poison gases such as hydrogen sulfide and carbon monoxide also seep out. These would kill almost every animal on the planet, but the mouth of the tube worm just takes it all in. This is no ordinary mouth. In fact, it doesn't swallow anything. Its bright red blood vessels absorb the gases directly. Once the poison gets into the tube worm's blood, the bacteria that live inside it do their work. They eat the poisons and secrete food directly into the worm's blood. That's right: the tube worm doesn't need a stomach—it's infected with bacteria that do its digesting for it. You know what that means, don't you? If you gave a tube worm some antibiotics, it would starve to death.

Dinner time!

Science or Fiction

For extra credit, answer the following question. Which of these examples is not a real animal?

(1) A BEEFALO
(the offspring of a bison and a cow)

(2) A ZEDONK
(the offspring of a donkey and a zebra)

(3) A CAMELOPARD
(half camel, half leopard)

The answer is:
None of the above . . . sort of! And if you answered *camelopard*, you're also right . . . sort of!

The first two are real animals with two different creatures for parents. The camelopard is an old name for a giraffe. In the 1700s, people thought that giraffes were too weird to be regular animals! They assumed the giraffe was a strange hybrid of a long-necked beast and something with spots. Even after the truth came out that giraffes give birth to other giraffes, some early zoologists still goofed up for a while—they started to argue that the *camelopard* and the giraffe must be two different species!

Zoinks! It's a zedonk!

I am not a camel

We don't know about you, but we think that's about as weird as the animal kingdom gets. Does it win your vote? If not, come up with your own candidate and write to us about it (see page 120). We're serious: if there's a creature weirder than that, we really want to know about it!

Bugs Rule!

We love bugs because they're small, creepy, and almost always weird. By bugs, we mean several classes of animals, none of which has a backbone. They include insects (creatures with six legs), arachnids (such as spiders, with eight legs), arthropods (multilegged creatures, like centipedes), and gastropods (things that slide around on their stomachs, like slugs and snails). If these critters ever declared war on humans, our best bet would be to surrender and bow to our new leaders before the first battle. In fact, no matter how many flyswatters, cans of bug spray, and citronella candles we might have, we'd be doomed from the outset. Why? Well, Earth is literally crawling with these guys. Bugs outnumber humans by millions to one, and there are more bugs per square mile in some forests than there are people on the whole planet! But they aren't just more numerous than us; they also have some scary powers and physical features.

SURRENDER PEACEFULLY!

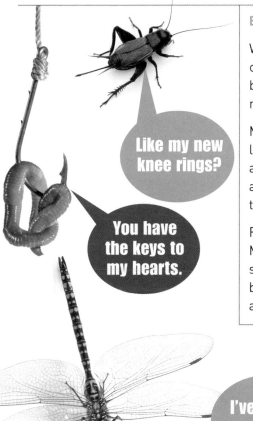

Like my new knee rings?

You have the keys to my hearts.

I've got my eyes on you!

Bug Bits

We know that insects have three times more legs than humans—and centipedes have even more. But did you know that bugs have lots of other extra body parts that humans don't? Worms have five hearts. Slugs have a ridiculous number of teeth: three thousand of them. They also have four noses.

Many insects have compound eyes—lots of little eyes clustered into groups that look like two eyes from a distance. Unlike humans, whose eyes face forward and work together to see things, bugs have eyes on both sides of their heads and see things from both sides. In the case of dragonflies, the placement of these eyes gives them a freaky power: they can see in all directions at once.

Forget what you've heard in Spider-Man movies. Spider senses aren't all that. Moth and cricket senses are much cooler. Moths have such a good sense of smell they can detect another moth from miles away. And crickets have a bizarre sense of hearing. It's not that it's so much better than that of other animals—it's where their ears are placed. Crickets hear through their knees.

I have a dentist appointment today.

You're gonna pay through the noses!

Lizard Lore

Salamanders have amazing healing powers. If a predator bites off a salamander's tail, it can grow back. So can its legs and eyes.

Chameleons are lizards that change color to blend in with their background. It's a kind of instant camouflage that makes it hard for predators to find them. If you take a chameleon out of a bush and stick it in a blue room, its skin will change from a green-brown pattern to blue in as little as twenty seconds.

Bug Olympics

Many bugs are incredibly strong and fast. Grasshoppers, for example, can jump better than Olympic athletes. If you scaled up a grasshopper to the same size as a human kid, it could clear a basketball court in a single bound. Ants are great weight lifters: they can carry fifty times their body weight—so if an ant was kid-sized, it could lift a car.

Bugs can swim better than humans, too. Cockroaches can be underwater for more than ten minutes without taking a breath.

We people do outperform some bugs, though. Take snails, for example. Snails crawl at about 220 hours a mile—not miles per hour, the other way around. If a snail crawled as fast as it could without stopping for nine straight days, it would travel only a single mile. Fortunately, it could take a nice rest afterward. Some snails can sleep for three years at a time.

I'll race you to the top of this page!

Bug Self-Defense

Skunks aren't the only creatures to give off bad smells when they're scared: ladybugs squirt smelly stuff from their knees to get rid of predators.

Some ants take self-defense to another level: they explode when predators attack. It doesn't save the ant being attacked—it's just blown itself to pieces, of course—but the experience sure scares the predators away from other ants in the colony.

Pee-Yew!

Bug Bashers

We can't hope to swat all the bugs in the world—or even in our backyards. Luckily, there are creatures that can help. Obviously, spiders do their part with their webs, but other bug-chugging creatures go in for bigger meals than your average arachnid. For instance, a bat can eat three thousand insects a night. Giant anteaters are even hungrier. They can eat more than thirty thousand insects a day. So don't freak out if you see bats flying around your neighborhood at night. They're just doing their part to keep the bug population down. If you see a giant anteater lumbering around in your backyard . . . feel free to freak out: they're up to eight feet long and live in South and Central America.

When you look up in the sky at sunset, you may be amazed to see a bat or two chomping on some bugs. Well, imagine seeing up to 100 million bats leave Tham Khang Khao (Bat Cave) in Thailand in search of food. They leave around 6 PM every evening and it takes two hours for all the bats to exit the cave.

Mega Stick Insects!

You see a lot of big bugs in science-fiction films, and there's a good reason for that. Up close, insects look very creepy. It's just as well that the biggest bug in the natural world is only about a foot long. But it's still a freaky-looking beast.

It's a stick insect called Chan's megastick, and it was discovered in 2008. The body of a Chan's megastick is fourteen inches long, but with its legs stretched out, it's about two feet long. That's not quite long enough to play stickball with, but it's still as long as a kid's arm!

It's not just the size of this insect that's weird. It hatches from an egg with two little wings on the sides—they look a bit like the golden snitch from the Harry Potter novels. When the wind blows through the forests of the megastick's native country, Borneo, it catches the egg wings and blows the eggs away to another tree. That way, wherever the newborn bug hatches out, it won't have to fight a lot of other megasticks for food.

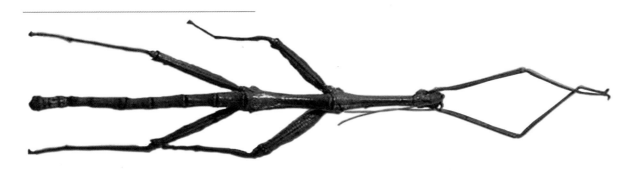

The First Animal to Walk the Earth

Scientists believe that marine life took its first steps on land about 360 million years ago. Fish had grown little legs and used them to push themselves across dry land. And one of the places it took those steps was on the north side of Route 120, near Hyner Run in Pennsylvania. Of course, things were very different back then. In fact, the land that is now northern Pennsylvania used to be a swamp south of the equator. But it was so nice, it could lure fish out of the water.

The fish in question is called a *hynerpeton*, named after the village of Hyner, where its fossil was found. The weird thing is that it wasn't found by a team of scientists but a team of road construction workers. They were digging the crumbly brown rock by the side of a road to make the road wider and stumbled across some strange fossils. Experts from the Academy of Natural Sciences in Philadelphia figured out that this fossil was one of the oldest amphibians in the world, and the first ever found in North America.

It was so old that Pennsylvania used to be almost 30 degrees south of the equator when hynerpeton walked the earth. This was 140 million years before the dinosaurs, when Pennsylvania was a tropical swamp full of strange life forms that flourished for a while and then died out. This crawling fish is a transitional life form, one that connects two distinct animal kingdoms. It's a missing link between water creatures and what we now know as amphibians. Its shoulder bone and fins show that the creature could propel itself through murky swamps and probably even grasp objects in its proto-fingers. Hynerpeton could pull itself out of the water and quite possibly breathe air.

Lovely day for a stroll...

She Sells Seashells

I sell seashells . . .

To understand the animal kingdom today, it really helps to study ancient animals that aren't around anymore. *Paleontology*—the study of ancient animal remains—started in England, where people collected fossils for fun in the 1700s and early 1800s. One of the most famous fossil hunters was a woman, Mary Anning, who supported her scientific work by selling spare fossils and shells. She was so well known, she inspired a tongue twister that speech therapists still torture people with—"she sells seashells by the seashore." (Seriously . . . we're not kidding!)

Mary Anning was also a dedicated scientist who introduced a new idea into paleontology: you can find out a lot about an extinct animal from studying what it left behind. She once found an interesting stone in a fossilized fish. It was a weird shape and seemed like an odd thing to be inside a fish, so

Even fossilized, this coprolite still looks like the real thing!

she broke it open. Inside the stone she found bones. At first, she called it a *bezoar* (pronounced *bee-zore*, a word that means any mass or stone you find in a body). After a while, she realized something gross and amazing at the same time: it was fossilized poop. It got a new name—*coprolite*.

The scientific world realized that coprolites could be really useful. You can determine what the animal ate by breaking open a coprolite and examining the contents. You can figure out what an animal's guts were like from a coprolite's shape. And you can tell who your friends are when you admit what you've been studying all day! Even now, paleontologists study fossilized poop. It's a dirty job, but someone's got to do it!

A collection of fossilized bezoars. Today, bezoars are considered undigested clumps of matter that accumulate in an animal's digestive system—sort of like a hair ball from a cat. They're used in Chinese medicine to remove poisons from the body. Harry Potter uses a bezoar from the stomach of a goat to save his friend Ron after he drank poison in *Harry Potter and the Half-Blood Prince*.

Two Heads Are Better than One

If you ever want to see a weird and wacky creature, all you need to do is turn on the TV or pop in a DVD of some crazy science-fiction flick. But back before movie special effects, people went to county fairs and paid a dime or a quarter to enter a sideshow tent to see their weird animals. Inside, you could see five-legged dogs, snakes with two heads, and other strange creatures. Many of these sideshow exhibits were fakes, but that doesn't mean they *all* were.

In fact, there are still many examples of animals so smart, they carry their extra brains in a backup head. You'll sometimes hear or read a news story about a cat or cow or snake being born with more than one head. It's a rare condition that occurs in many animals, and it's called *polycephaly*. For many years, the San Francisco Academy of Sciences had a live two-headed snake. But most two-headed animals don't live long lives, so it's rare to find a live example. However, lots of natural history buffs and fans of the weird want to see them, so many are stuffed and mounted by taxidermists and put on display. If you're lucky, you might be able to find one near you.

Several branches of Ripley's Believe It or Not! Museum still have stuffed calves with two heads (Gatlinburg, Tennessee, and Ocean City, Maryland, both have one). And a couple of local museums can make similar boasts.

The Georgia State Capitol in Atlanta has a full-body taxidermy of a two-faced kitten and a head mount of a two-headed calf. Full-body stuffed two-headed calves are fairly common. There are examples at Douglas County Museum in Waterville, Washington; Dalton Gang Hideout Museum in Meade, Kansas; the Ohio Historical Society; and Joseph Steward's Museum of Natural and Other Curiosities, in the Old State House in Hartford, Connecticut. You can probably find photos of polycephaly on the Web, too, but most of the examples we've found are obvious fakes, so you're better off sticking with the real deal.

Oh, and if two-headed animals creep you out, how about five-legged ones? Fivey, the five-legged dog, was a local Baltimore favorite for years until the museum its stuffed body lived in closed down. It's now on display in a club called The Palace of Wonders in Washington, D.C.

Two quacks are better than one.

Moo moo.

Who Needs a Brain?

Not every living creature has a head or a brain. Bacteria, jellyfish, and viruses do fine without them. But as a general rule, if you're born with a backbone, you need a head at the top of it to stay alive. "Ah," you may say, "what about chickens? They can run around after they've had their heads cut off."

It's true, but a headless chicken's last run is really just a dying animal's legs twitching. Most of the time, headless chickens run about for a few minutes, then they fall over and become dinner. But there's one famous exception to this rule: the story of farmer Lloyd Olsen's chicken, Mike.

Spotty's Calf

Spotty's two-headed calf was born in Brookville, Ohio, in 1941 on the farm of Wilbur and Nettie Rasor. It died soon after, but the Rasors had it stuffed and charged folks a dime to visit. (Residents of Brookville recall Wilbur coming into town to buy a new car with buckets of dimes.) When the Rasors purchased a live four-horned, four-eyed, two-nosed bull and added it to the exhibit, they raised admission to a quarter.

Farmer Olsen whacked an ax at Mike back in 1945, ready to turn him into dinner. After his head came off, Mike walked about a bit as the farmer waited for him to stop. He kept waiting until bedtime, and Mike was still moving. Farmer Olsen left him in his coop and went to bed. The next day, he found Mike asleep with his neck under his wing.

Olsen figured anything that was determined to live without a head deserved a chance. So he got an eyedropper and dropped grain and water down Mike's neck. Mike's wounds healed and still he went on walking.

The residents of Fruita, Colorado, soon started to visit Olsen's farm to see Mike strut his headless stuff. For twenty-five cents, Farmer Olsen would let them in. Soon, he started to attract magazines and newspapers, and Miracle Mike the Headless Chicken became a tourist attraction. People flocked in from all over the country to see him. *The Guinness Book of World Records* wrote him up, and in the wave of publicity, Farmer Olsen decided to insure Mike's life for ten thousand dollars. That's a lot of McNuggets!

Scientists at the University of Utah figured out how Mike survived. Farmer Olsen's ax had missed Mike's jugular vein, so he hadn't bled to death. He'd also swung a bit low, and that had left Mike's brain stem intact. A brain stem is all the brain a chicken really needs to keep breathing and moving, so after Mike's cuts had healed up, he could carry on as normal—as long as someone kept feeding him. Farmer Olsen was only too glad to oblige.

Mike the Headless Chicken led a full and productive life for another two years, when he choked on some grain and passed on. But that's not the end of Mike's story. After fifty years, the town of Fruita, where Mike came from, decided to celebrate its most famous headless hero. Beginning in 1998, the city has held an annual party called Mike the Headless Chicken Day. On the third weekend in May, the townsfolk gather and compete in Chicken Dance contests and a 5K Run Like a Headless Chicken race.

You can read more on Mike's website, www.miketheheadlesschicken.org . . . because every headless chicken deserves its own website, don't you think?

Fruita, Colorado, celebrates Mike the Headless Chicken Day each May. If you attend, don't forget to stop off at the sculpture of Mike in the center of town.

Fact or Fake?

Now that you've dived deep into the world of weird animals, do you reckon you can tell the difference between real animals and fakes? Take a look at these examples of strange creatures from around the United States (and its coastal waters). Do they look real or fake to you?

Jackalope

What looks like a jackrabbit, hops like a jackrabbit, and has horns like an antelope? A jackalope, of course! The Wichita Art Museum and the University of Kansas Natural History Museum have stuffed jackalopes, and we've seen a few others in sideshows.

Is it real or fake? Before you answer, look for a clue in the previous paragraph. See it? It's the bit about the art museum. What would a real animal be doing in an art museum?

Yep, the jackalope is an example of what carnival operators call "gaffs"—creative fakes put together by clever artists. Instead of doing what taxidermists usually do—simply prepare dead animals for display—they use authentic animal parts from several different animals and make a Frankenstein's monster out of them. But people still swear they've seen jackalopes in the wild. It's probably a strange illness that makes cottontail rabbits look as though they have horns: biologists Richard E. Shope and W. W. Hurst discovered a virus that makes rabbits' skin swell, sometimes to antler-like size. So it seems that sometimes science can be weirder than creative taxidermists.

Furry Fish

Tales of strange-looking fish with furry bodies have spread through many cold areas in the United States. They say that trout survive in the freezing waters of Montana, Wyoming, and Colorado by growing a thick layer of fur in wintertime. Now that we've told you about creative taxidermy, you've probably already guessed that the furry fish is a fake. Fish don't grow fur, even in cold climates. The story may have started as a joke or it may have been a genuine misunderstanding—there is a fungus that grows on some sick fish that looks like hair—but every example that's stuffed and mounted in a museum is a fake.

FUR BEARING TROUT
Very Rare
Caught while fishing in GREAT SLAVE LAKE near YELLOWKNIFE, NWT
It is believed that the great depth and extreme penetrating coldness
of the water in which these fish live has caused them to grow
their dense coat of "unusualb" white fur.

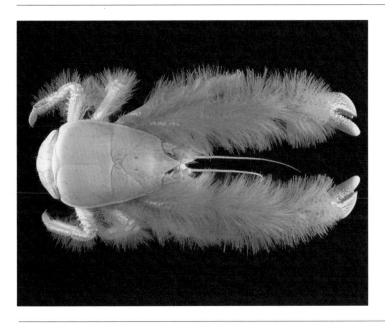

Yeti Crab

We heard a strange story about a research project led by the Monterey Bay Aquarium Research Institute in California. They went deep into the Pacific Ocean, down where underwater volcanoes send toxic gases into the water. There, they found an animal they called the yeti crab, a white, six-inch-long crab with fur all over its pincers. The fur was covered with bacteria and smaller animals.

So is the yeti crab real or fake? It's real, but the fur isn't! These strands aren't real hair, but the crab needs them to survive. Scientists speculate that the bacteria that live in the strands filter out the poisons in the nasty water down there, and possibly provide food for this creepy creature.

THE MAD SCIENTISTS

none of the scientists in this chapter was actually truly mad. Yet they all had a weird side. Thomas Edison was responsible for more than a thousand inventions, but he also tried to create a spirit phone to talk to dead people. Nikola Tesla came up with AC (or alternating current), the type of electrical power that we use to power our homes, but he also claimed to have invented a device through which he could communicate with extraterrestrials. We like to think that their weird sides helped these scientists accomplish great things. Who knows? Perhaps genius and weirdness go together and wild imagination and crazy inspiration are part of the scientific process. We can't say for sure, but with this chapter we'd like to pay tribute to the weirder sides of some very brilliant and very strange scientists.

Alexander Fleming, the Germ Painter

"We all know that chance, fortune, fate, or destiny—call it what you will—has played a considerable part in many of the great discoveries in science."—Dr. Alexander Fleming, accepting the Nobel Prize for Medicine in 1945

Every time you get treated for an ear infection, say a quiet "thank you" to Dr. Alexander Fleming. This smart Scotsman studied bacteria, the nasty little germs that give you infections, and accidentally found a cure for them. As part of his job studying bacteria, he had to grow them in dishes. He'd drip the bacteria onto bacteria food—a jelly called *agar*—and wait for them to multiply. Bacteria are too small to see, but millions of bacteria in one spot *can* be seen. And after a few days on the jelly, Dr. Fleming would see the clear drips change color. He'd then know he had plenty of bacteria to study.

At one time in the 1920s, Dr. Fleming left out his bacteria dishes too long, and mold started to grow on the jelly. But he decided it didn't matter that much—he'd try to grow bacteria on it anyway. The bacteria did grow, but it stayed away from the mold. This led Dr. Fleming to think that mold must have something in it that killed bacteria. He extracted that chemical from the mold, called it *penicillin*, and invented the antibiotic. Doctors have been prescribing the stuff ever since. This accidental discovery has saved millions of lives and given much relief to people with aching ears!

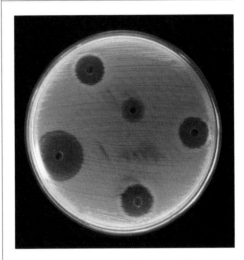

Antibiotics being tested in a petri dish.

All serious medical students know about Alexander Fleming the scientist, but they don't know the other side of this great man. He used bacteria for his hobby, too. He was an amateur painter; however, instead of paint, he used germs. During his day job, he'd found out that one sort of bacteria (*serratia marcescens*) was a nice red color, another (*chromobacterium violaceum*) was purple, and various micrococcus bacteria were yellow, white, and pink. And *bacillus sp.* was an attractive orange color. So he'd draw pictures, paint them with bacteria, and wait for them to grow.

So don't let anyone say that science and art don't mix. They mix up just fine, even if the results are kind of weird.

We're glad Fleming didn't give up his day job . . . for many reasons!

His Brain Was Open

Paul Erdos (1913–1996) published more than any other mathematician in history. All in all, he wrote more than 1,500 papers, books, and articles. (Most mathematicians would be happy with twenty or thirty!) How did Paul Erdos accomplish so much? He collaborated with hundreds of different people all around the world. Here's how it worked: A legendary eccentric, Erdos lived out of a suitcase. He'd show up at a colleague's doorstep and announce, "My brain is open." He'd move in for a while, write a few papers with his friend, and then move on.

For Erdos, math wasn't something you did alone in your room. It was a social activity to be done with close friends while you're eating their food and sleeping in their guest room. Erdos developed a unique vocabulary to match his odd personality. As you'd expect, many of the phrases he invented pertained to math.

All epsilons should know their multiplication tables!

- "My brain is open," was Erdos-speak for, "Let's do math together."

- "To exist" was to work as a mathematician, and "to die" was to stop doing math.

- He referred to children as "epsilons," because, in mathematics, the Greek letter epsilon refers to a small positive quantity. Meanwhile, men were "slaves" and women were "bosses."

As a fitting tribute, mathematicians assign Erdos numbers as a measurement of collaboration. If you collaborated with Erdos directly, your Erdos number would be 1. If you collaborated with someone who collaborated with Erdos, then you'd get a 2. If you collaborated with someone who collaborated with someone who collaborated with Erdos, then you'd get a 3, and so on, and so on. Erdos numbers have been given not only to mathematicians but also to actors, a baseball player, a baby, and a horse. But there's only one person with an Erdos number of 0. That would be Paul Erdos himself.

Edison vs. Tesla

Few scientists have shaped the modern world more than Thomas Alva Edison (1847–1931) and Nikola Tesla (1856–1943). When you switch on a light, you can give a shout-out to Edison. (No! He didn't invent the lightbulb, but he was responsible for the first reliable, inexpensive, long-lasting electric lights.) When you plug in a toaster or a computer, you can thank Tesla. (He developed alternating current, which is how our homes receive electrical power.) Edison had more than one thousand inventions to his name. He was the first scientist to successfully record and play back sound, and he was instrumental in the birth of movies. Tesla invented modern radio. The Serbian scientist also was responsible for the Tesla coil, a neat device that amateur science lovers often use to create wild, sparking, electrical demonstrations.

Now you'd think two great minds like these would be pals; however, the two inventors were enemies. (Tesla had worked for Edison at one point and claimed that the inventor had stiffed him on a paycheck.) They also had very different working methods. Edison's approach involved trial and error and countless hours of hard work. As he famously put it, "Genius is 1 percent inspiration, 99 percent perspiration." Tesla felt that, if Edison upped the inspiration a bit, then maybe he wouldn't have to sweat so much. "A little theory and calculation would have saved him 90 percent of his labor," said Tesla about his former boss. Now, that may seem a harmless thing to say, but to scientists, those are fighting words!

We won't attempt to compare the accomplishments of these two titans of science. Instead, we'll suggest another sort of contest: Who was weirder—Edison or Tesla?

Edison, the Electrocuter

Edison's inventions ran on direct current, or DC. Tesla had developed alternating current—or AC—for Edison's rival, George Westinghouse, of the Westinghouse Electric & Manufacturing Company. Feeling threatened by Westinghouse, Edison wanted to smash AC in favor of DC, so he started a battle known as "the War of the Currents." To show that AC was dangerous, Edison sponsored AC electrocutions of cats, dogs, and, most famously, a circus elephant named Topsy, who had run amuck and killed a few people. When publicizing these events, Edison wouldn't use the word *electrocute*. He preferred saying that the animals had been "Westinghoused." Edison's obsession led to one invention he wasn't all that proud of: the electric chair. If you're wondering who won the war of the currents, remember that your home uses AC. That's right! This is one battle that Edison lost.

Tesla, why don't you go play with your pigeons!

Hey, Edison, you owe me. Pay up!

Cool as a cucumber, Tesla reads by the light of his awesome lightning-producing Tesla coil.

Tesla, the Germophobic, Pigeon-loving, Pearl-hater

Tesla was desperately afraid of germs and dirt. (For you lovers of weird words, the fear of germs and dirt is called *mysophobia*.) He hated human hair, round objects, jewelry, and particularly pearl earrings. He liked the number 3 (he always demanded to be placed in hotel rooms with numbers divisible by 3) and absolutely adored pigeons. Toward the end of his life, he obsessively cared for the pigeons that he fed in Central Park in New York City. Injured birds would get special treatment. He'd take them back to his hotel room and attend to them until they were well again.

Edison, the Man of Concrete

After opening a cement plant in Stewartsville, New Jersey, Edison forged ahead on a project that, understandably, never quite took off. He wanted to mass-produce inexpensive, concrete houses. Additional furnishings included concrete bathtubs, concrete cabinets, and, for the musically inclined, concrete pianos. Using an enormous house-sized mold, the cement would be poured, and less than a week later, a fireproof home was ready to be lived in. Unfortunately, Edison didn't foresee a major problem: concrete houses are ugly. On the positive side, they're durable. You can see the results for yourself if you visit Union, New Jersey. Some of the cement homes he built there are still standing, looking as ugly as ever after almost a hundred years.

Tesla, the Mad, Mad, Mad, Mad Scientist

Tesla dreamed of building a camera for photographing thoughts. (Not sure what our brains would project: Question marks? Singing space aliens? Dancing Bigfoot?) He wanted to build a gigantic tower that would harvest cosmic rays and distribute free energy to everyone on the planet. He thought of building remote-control flying saucers and a "teleforce" super weapon, which was a charged beam splitter that could electrocute an army from two hundred miles away. (At the time, some journalists called it a peace ray. Others dubbed it a death ray.) And some say that he succeeded in building an interplanetary communication device called the Teslascope.

This cool gadget is known as a Tesla Plasma Ball Globe. Touch and sound make the bolts of light dance inside the glass.

One of Edison's heavy homes.

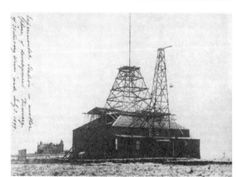

Tesla's mad scientist lab in Colorado Springs, Colorado.

Edison, the Paranormalist

In his later years, Edison reportedly worked on a spirit phone to communicate with the dead. (If he had succeeded, we would have tried to arrange a person-to-dead-person interview with Edison himself!) He also conducted a wacky paranormal experiment. Fooled by a self-proclaimed mind reader named Bert Reese (who was later exposed as a fraud by Harry Houdini), Edison wrapped electric coils around his head and the heads of three other colleagues who were stationed at various locations within the same house. The four men then tried to communicate telepathically. Later Edison commented, "We achieved no result in mind reading."

Tesla, the . . . Venusian

Tesla himself would be weirded out by this one! In 1971, a strange book was written by Arthur H. Matthews, a man who claimed to have once worked with Tesla. The title was *The Wall of Light: Nikola Tesla & the Venusian Space Ship, the X-12*. According to Matthews, Tesla was born on the planet Venus and was brought to Earth on the X-12, a spaceship that traveled by "thought projection."

Hello? I'm trying to reach Leonardo da Vinci. He's not home? Can I leave a message?

From *The Wall of Light*:

"We know that space ships have landed on earth, all through the ages. Tesla said that he believed he came from the planet Venus, and during the landings of a space ship on my property, the members of that ship said that Tesla was a child from Venus."

And the Winner Is . . .

Whew! And the winner of our "Who is weirder?" contest is . . . Tesla! He wasn't from Venus, of course, but for having inspired such lunacy, he's a hard (mad)man to beat. If we get a spirit phone call from Edison demanding a rematch, we'll let you know.

A Weird Central Winner?

We here on

VENUS

are sure proud of cousin

NIKOLA

Antigravity's Outcast

With stories linking Tesla to flying saucers and interplanetary phone calls, it's not surprising that the Serbian scientist has become a hero to conspiracy theorists and UFO buffs around the globe. Yet, in weird-science circles, there's another, less familiar name that keeps popping up. Unlike Tesla, Thomas Townsend Brown (1905–1985) is rarely mentioned in science books. In fact, for the most part, the man is virtually unknown, even within the science community.

Why is Brown a legend only to enthusiasts of the weird? The answer becomes clear when you learn the subject of his research: antigravity!

Brown grew up in Zanesville, Ohio. Even as a boy, he was curious and inventive. We've heard rumors about some of his early creations—an umbrella wired to receive radio broadcasts, a clubhouse rigged with a voice-activated lightbulb. We have no idea if these tales are true, but it's safe to say that T. T. Brown was a smart kid.

Brown hated studying but loved fooling around with electricity. After struggling as a student for many years, he eventually wound up working at Denison University in Granville, Ohio, with a scientist named Paul Biefeld. Brown was experimenting with capacitors (electrical components that can hold and give off charge, like batteries) when he discovered something odd. Sending a high voltage through a capacitor, Brown noticed that the capacitor jumped. He didn't understand why it moved, but he was convinced that he'd found a link between electricity and gravity. Giving his teacher a little credit, he called the phenomenon the Biefeld-Brown Effect, and he proudly announced the birth of a strange new field: *electrogravatics*.

Shortly afterward, he started making weird, levitating gadgets called *gravitators*. In a 1929 *Science and Invention* article entitled "How I Control Gravity," Brown imagined a future where enormous gravitators would drive ocean liners and guide "space cars" all the way to Mars.

Soon, he was putting on wild demonstrations with flying saucer–shaped capacitors. With wires, he connected these gravitators to a pole, which served as their power source. When he turned on the juice, the disks would rise and begin whizzing around the pole. (Imagine the Invisible Man playing T-Ball with a flying saucer and you'll get the picture.)

What happened next? Strange as it may seem, Brown's discoveries were generally disregarded, and the man became an outcast, not a hero. More and more, his name became connected with flying saucers, not science. (And it didn't help when, in 1956, he founded a UFO organization called the National Investigations Committee on Aerial Phenomena [NICAP]. Bad career move for a scientist!)

T. T. Brown with one of his flying-saucer gravitators.

Over time, Brown found it harder to convince investors to fund his work. Yet he never stopped believing in electrogravatics and he never stopped being curious. In the 1980s, just before he died, he was still tinkering with electricity, trying to measure the charge given off by sand and various rocks.

Why was his work dismissed? Conspiracy theorists insist that Brown had figured out the science behind UFOs. They believe that the government swatted down Brown's electrogravatics as part of a big UFO cover-up. Scientists offer a more plausible explanation for why electrogravatics never took off. The theory is that Brown's flying saucers levitate because of a known phenomenon called "ion wind," which is a strong wind produced by an electric field. Without air, you can't have ion wind, and so, in space, where there is no air, Brown's saucers could never fly. In summary: Brown's demonstrations were cool, but his saucers weren't antigravity machines. They were just electrically operated hovercrafts and would never have made it to Mars.

End of story? Not quite. We won't be traveling through space on antigravity ships powered by gravitators, but that doesn't mean that Brown's discovery doesn't have a future. Recently, science hobbyists have started building their own levitating machines based on the Biefeld-Brown effect. These devices aren't called gravitators anymore, because we know they are not really defying gravity. Instead, they're known as lifters or ionocrafts or beamships (because they're made of beams of balsa wood). And they're so simple to build that they've become a popular project for school science fairs. If you ever decide to build your own beamship, make sure to spread the word about its inventor, Thomas Townsend Brown. It's about time people remembered the scientist for more than just his weird side!

A Tale of Two Paleontologists

There's nothing wrong with a little friendly competition, but the rivalry between Edward Drinker Cope and Othniel Charles Marsh was anything but. In fact, we can't think of two scientists who have hated each other more than these two paleontologists did.

Paleontology, the study of prehistoric life, became a hot topic after the first nearly complete dinosaur skeleton was found in a marlstone pit in Haddonfield, New Jersey, in 1858. The new science attracted all sorts of people from a wide range of backgrounds.

Cope came from money. He was self-taught, hot-tempered, and impulsive. Marsh's family was less wealthy, but he received a superior university education. He was slower and more thoughtful than Cope. To Cope, Marsh was an arrogant, low-class bumpkin. To Marsh, Cope was a rich slacker, spoiled and unprofessional.

My brain is bigger than yours, Marsh.

Oh, Cope, get a life, already.

Despite their differences, the two men got along at first, and even collected fossils together. Then Marsh got sneaky. He bribed the owner of a pit, requesting that all fossils be sent to him, not Cope. Cope discovered the ploy and began to distrust his cohort. Making matters worse, Marsh embarrassed Cope by pointing out a silly mistake he'd made on an elasmosaurus skeleton. In a rush, Cope had mixed up the neck and the tail, and so the dinosaur's head was perched on the wrong end. Cope felt humiliated, and distrust turned to hatred. From then on, it was a no-holds-barred fight to the finish.

The fierce competition between the two rival paleontologists lasted for more than twenty years. And they often played dirty. Marsh stole fossils from Cope, and Cope stole fossils from Marsh. They attacked each other in print and they spied on each other. If one heard about a fossil site, he'd race to claim it first. Then he'd plunder and destroy it, leaving the other with nothing to sift through but a pile of fossil rubble.

Bribery. Name-calling. Nothing was too underhanded for these two reckless, ruthless scientists. Their battle became known as the "Bone Wars." (The feud could have had a catchier name, don't you think? The Ferocious Fossil Fight? The Dastardly Dinosaur Dispute?) The contest led to many scientific breakthroughs. Before Cope and Marsh began fighting, only nine species of dinosaurs were known. By the time the Bone Wars ended, the number had swelled to more than two hundred! The discoveries of Cope and Marsh led to dinosaur skeletons in museums across the country, and dinosaur-mania in the hearts of children all over the world.

Couldn't you guys just share? There's enough for everyone!

One of Cope's quarry sites.

This photograph shows Marsh with one of his digging teams. Notice they're holding guns and not shovels? Fossil hunting was dangerous business during the feud.

On the negative side, in their attempts to sabotage each other, Cope and Marsh destroyed worthwhile fossil sites. Besides, the long, expensive battle left both scientists almost completely broke.

But even when poverty-stricken and on his deathbed in 1897, Cope refused to give up the fight. In his will, he requested that his brain be removed and measured, and he challenged his opponent to a brain-to-brain standoff to see whose was bigger. Marsh refused.

Who won the Bone Wars? Scientifically speaking, it's a silly question, since both men made giant contributions to the field of paleontology. But we at Weird Central love answering silly questions, so we dug up the numbers and confirmed that Cope discovered fifty-six new species of dinosaurs. Marsh discovered eighty. However, it seems that Marsh mistakenly double-counted. He counted the brontosaurus and the apatosaurus as two separate beasts, but scientists say that they are the same, and so brontosauruses had to be removed from school textbooks. (Sorry, brontosaurus lovers! Get yourselves a new favorite dinosaur!) More recently, some paleontologists have claimed that the triceratops and the torosaurus are the same as well.

First the brontosaurus! Now the triceratops! With Marsh losing points, is there a chance that Cope will catch up? Nope! The Bone Wars are over, and Marsh won!

An illustration from one of Cope's articles. The head of the elasmosaurus (the creature in the water in the foreground) is shown on the wrong end—a fact Marsh was more than happy to point out. Cope spent a lot of money buying up every copy of the magazine in which this article and illustration appeared.

The Drinker and the Othnielia

The plant-eating *drinker* is a dinosaur named after Edward Drinker Cope. The lightning-fast *othnielia* was named after Othniel Charles Marsh. These small, bird-footed dinosaurs lived during the Late Jurassic Period, about 150 million years ago. We're not sure if they existed at the same time, but if they did, we hope that the drinker and the othnielia got along better than their human counterparts.

On the Road with Einstein's Brain

Like most people, Albert Einstein had a weird side. But this little tale isn't about the brilliant physicist's eccentricities. Instead, our story begins on April 18, 1955, after Einstein died at Princeton Hospital in New Jersey.

Dr. Thomas Stoltz Harvey worked in the hospital at the time as a pathologist. (A forensic pathologist is a physician who performs autopsies on corpses in order to diagnose diseases and help determine the cause of death.) In the event of his death, Einstein had wanted his remains to be cremated. He had never agreed to an autopsy. Ignoring these minor details, Dr. Harvey performed an autopsy on Einstein anyway. He must have been overcome by the thought of personally examining one of the greatest minds of all time.

The pathologist removed Einstein's brain and carefully cut it into 240 blocks. He gave some of the blocks away and stored the leftover brain chunks in two mason jars full of formalin, a preservative. He wasn't interested in Einstein's eyes, so he let Einstein's eye doctor take them. (Years later, the eye doctor, Henry Abrams, considered selling the eyes, and singer Michael Jackson reportedly offered $5 million. The sale never happened, and the eyes are supposedly still in a bank vault in New York City.)

Here's where the story gets weird. Harvey took Einstein's brain home with him. Princeton Hospital demanded that he return the organ, but he refused. So, he was fired. Harvey and his wife had

STOLEN!

ONE GENIUS BRAIN

REWARD

IF RETURNED TO OWNER.

fights about the brain and eventually separated. We've heard that Mrs. Harvey even threatened to throw the brain in the trash, but fortunately this never happened. Dr. Thomas Stoltz Harvey snatched Einstein's brain and hit the road.

Lugging the brain from place to place, he relocated often, frequently distributing brain samples to researchers so that they could be studied. In 1978, a journalist found Harvey in Wichita, Kansas, and confirmed that the preserved brain chunks were safe and sound (still floating in mason jars, which were packed away in a cardboard box). By the 1990s, Dr. Harvey had grown weary of Einstein's burdensome brain. Placing the cardboard box in the trunk of his Buick, he set off from his new home in New Jersey and traveled across the country with a freelance writer documenting the trip. In California, Harvey tried to hand over the brain to Einstein's granddaughter, but she didn't want it.

In 1996, he returned to Princeton Hospital and gave the precious jars to a doctor who worked at Harvey's old job, pathologist Dr. Elliot Krauss. "Eventually, you get tired of the responsibility of having it," commented Harvey.

Studies done on Einstein's brain have been inconclusive. But one researcher noted a high number of glial cells. Glial cells provide nutrients to neurons in the brain. We're not sure what all this means; it sounds like Einstein's brain wasn't uncommonly large, but still it required a heck of a lot of maintenance. As the brain's faithful, devoted caretaker for more than forty years, Dr. Harvey might agree.

Albert Einstein in 1947, with his brain still attached.

To get kids interested in science, Dean Kamen started an organization called FIRST (For Inspiration and Recognition of Science and Technology). FIRST holds annual competitions in Lego-building and robotics. If you're a Lego master or an aspiring robot maker, or if you just love science and want to get involved, you can check out www.usfirst.org for details.

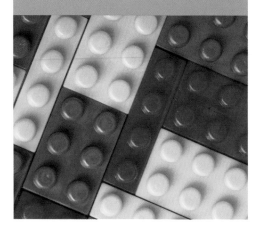

Lord Dumpling of North Dumpling Island

Dean Kamen and the Segway are the perfect pairing of weird inventor and weird invention. The Segway looks like a pogo stick on wheels. A self-balancing scooter, it moves forward if you lean forward and backs up when you lean back, and it always looks like it's about to topple, but it never does. It somehow seems to defy gravity. The secret of the Segway involves gyroscopic sensors in the base. We won't go into details, but the force behind gyroscopes is the same as the force that keeps a spinning top from falling over.

The Segway is an incredibly cool device, yet whenever we see someone riding one, we burst out laughing. Is it just us, or is there something hysterically funny about the sight of someone whizzing down the street on a Segway? In his own odd way, the scientist behind the Segway is every bit as weird as his creation. Even weirder.

A prolific inventor, Dean Kamen is also responsible for many breakthrough medical devices like robotic wheelchairs controlled by brainpower. His primary residence in Bedford, New Hampshire, is a surreal, hexagon-shaped wonderland with secret passages and hallways that look like mine shafts. Affectionately called Westwind, it's where Kamen keeps his collection of antique wheelchairs as well as his two helicopters. (He flies to work in the morning, often blasting the *Star Wars* soundtrack.)

The Segway in action.

Still, it is Kamen's second home that truly shows off his weird side. In 1986, he purchased one of two Dumpling Islands, located in the Fisher Island Sound, off the coast of Connecticut. On North Dumpling Island, the scientist has built a replica of Stonehenge. As you've probably guessed by now, Dean Kamen doesn't think small.

Kamen's dream was to power his private island entirely with energy from the wind and the sun. Early on, he encountered a problem: the local government informed Kamen that he couldn't put a windmill on his property. The inventor fought back with humor and quite a bit of eccentricity. Jokingly, he announced that North Dumpling Island had seceded from the United States. Kamen gave his new kingdom its own constitution, its own national anthem, and its own flag. As ruler of North Dumpling Island, he adopted the nickname Lord Dumpling. Instead of U.S. dollars, Kamen declared that the currency of North Dumpling Island would be the "Dumpling." He even drafted a Dumpling bill. It's not worth 5 or 10 Dumplings. Instead he picked a number, which in mathematics is represented by a Greek letter: pi.

Eventually Lord Dumpling won the battle of North Dumpling Island. Bypassing electric companies, Dean Kamen gets all the power he needs to light his island from wind generators, solar panels, and energy-saving LED lights.

For budding mathematicians, pi is a very important number. The first fifty digits are 3.14 15926535897932384626433 83327950288419716939937 5105820974944592, but the number keeps going on and on after that, out to infinity. Memorizing all of it would be impossible, and so Dean Kamen's Pi Dumpling bill is easily the world's weirdest and most useless currency. Also, since the first three digits of pi are 3.14, March 14 is Pi Day. If you're reading this on March 14, have a very happy Pi Day! And if you're reading this on March 14 and it's also your birthday, we hope you don't mind sharing your big day with a mathematical constant.

Lord Dumpling's domain.

$\pi = 3.14159265358979323846264338327950288419...$

CRAZY CHEMISTRY

We here at Weird Central love chemistry. Mixing chemicals feels dangerous, even if it's in controlled experiments in the science lab (or kitchen), and some of our favorite playthings are just weird chemistry experiments gone wrong. (We're thinking of Silly Putty and other goopy things that science created, couldn't use, and gave to kids to play with.) In fact, all the weird things in the world around us are made of chemicals—even the weirdos around us!

When we're feeling especially weird, we like to reel off the names of our favorite chemicals. For example, on a hot summer day, there's nothing we like better than to ingest sweet molecules of galactose, glucose, and sucrose, frozen in a suspension with triglyceride lipids, calcium, and our favorite globulin—that's lactoglobulin, of course! Mmmm! Just thinking about it makes us hungry! You'd prefer to chow down on ice cream? Well, that's what we just said!

The amazing thing about chemicals is that everything we know is made of them, and all the chemicals in the world are made up of just over one hundred elements. Our favorite candy chemical, chocolate, is made of theobromine. And theobromine is made of four elements: carbon, nitrogen, hydrogen, and oxygen. Guess what? So's the air you breathe!

The atmosphere contains carbon, nitrogen, hydrogen, and oxygen, too! With every breath you take, you gulp in lots of these things into your lungs. But they don't taste like chocolate. The big difference between chocolate and the atmosphere is the way those four elements are put together. You can't breathe chocolate! You can't eat air! But they're all made of the same stuff.

Yep, we here at Weird Central like our chemicals, and as a branch of Weird Science, chemistry is one of our favorites. All kinds of weird scientists have dabbled in chemistry, and here are some of the results they turned up.

The Search for the Philosopher's Stone

Chemistry is the only branch of science that was once officially a type of magic. Thousands of years ago, what we know as science was called "natural philosophy," and it was a mixture of scientific thinking and religious beliefs. Astronomers named the planets after their gods. Some of them believed that the movements of the planets affected us on Earth— that's where astrology and horoscopes come from. But even stranger than astrologers were the alchemists. More than two thousand years ago, these strange sort-of scientists believed that messing about with chemicals could turn lead into gold and help humans live forever. They thought that a magic rock called the Philosopher's Stone could help them reach both of these goals, and they spent centuries experimenting, searching, and exchanging secret formulas in their quest.

Yep, alchemists had some weird ideas, but these weird ideas drove them to create the methods that chemists still use today. Alchemists heated, evaporated, and distilled various substances; they took really good notes; and they kept on experimenting. Yes, many alchemists acted like real scientists. In fact, one alchemist is revered today as the father of modern science. Back in the 1600s, Isaac Newton, the man who discovered gravity and many other laws of physics, conducted hundreds of alchemy experiments and wrote them up in secret. His alchemy papers became public less than a hundred years ago, and they shed new light on the scientist and on alchemy itself. Up until the news about Newton, most modern people believed alchemists were all frauds.

Back in the 1300s, a storyteller named Geoffrey Chaucer wrote "The Canon's Yeoman's Tale," which explains how a cheating alchemist hollowed out a lump of coal, filled it with silver powder, and plugged the hole with wax. Then he tricked people into thinking he could make silver from a few powders. He lit a fire with the fake coal in it, and the heat melted the wax plug and real silver trickled out at the bottom of the fire. He tricked a lot of people out of their money with this nifty trick.

The true portraiture of GEFFREY CHAUCER the famous English poet, as by THOMAS OCCLEUE is described who liued in his time, and was his Scholar.

SIR ISAAC NEWTON

Newton's Follies

Newton is remembered as one of the world's most influential scientists and mathematicians; however, Newton was more interested in the occult and alchemy. He spent a lot of time trying to discover the Elixir of Life, a drink that gave one eternal life; he believed metals "possessed a sort of life"; he stated that the world would certainly end, but no earlier than 2060; and finally, he believed he had been chosen by God to be a prophet.

The Alchemist's Code

Alchemists were magical thinkers who believed that everything on Earth was ruled by planets and stars. They identified seven metals we recognize today—gold, silver, mercury, copper, iron, tin, and lead—and they named them after objects in the sky, because they believed that planets and stars affected them.

Gold – Sun

Silver – The Moon

Mercury – Mercury

Copper – Venus

Iron – Mars

Tin – Jupiter

Lead – Saturn

Quicksilver, otherwise known as mercury.

Does this sound weird? It shouldn't—the alchemists' odd ideas gave mercury its name. Most English-speaking people called it quicksilver, but the alchemists' mystical ideas won out!

The Last Known Location of the Philosopher's Stone

Some people believe that the Philosopher's Stone lies at the bottom of a river near Philadelphia. A group of hermits who lived near the Wissahickon River in the 1600s had a strange reputation. They were college-educated Germans who practiced medicine, studied the stars, and wrote hymns for the good people of Philadelphia. Their leader, Johannes Kelpius, has a legend associated with him. As he lay dying, he asked an assistant to throw his box of secrets into the

Alchemists working on creating the Philosopher's Stone.

Wissahickon. His assistant believed that the box contained the legendary Philosopher's Stone, and he was tempted to keep it, so that Kelpius's secrets could live on in their community. So he hid the box, went back to his master, and lied to him. Kelpius knew right away that the box wasn't in the river, and he told his assistant to do the job properly. When the box hit the water, the sky darkened, thunder rumbled, and lightning flew around the river. Kelpius knew that his magical secrets were sinking to the bottom of the river and died in peace.

Chewable Chemistry

One of our favorite chemicals is one we're not allowed to take to school. It's *polyethylene*. This stretchy, chewy, never-dissolving stuff goes by another name: chewing gum. And we stick it in our mouths nowadays because between 2,000 and 1,200 years ago, three different cultures chewed another chemical. They found theirs in a rubbery sap from trees: the Mayans chewed sapodilla tree sap; the ancient Greeks chomped on sap from the mastic tree; and in northern America, many tribes kept their jaws going for hours with the sap of the spruce tree. The sap of all these trees dries to a solid at room temperature, but the heat inside the mouth melts it down to a rubbery texture, and the mild taste and sheer fun of chewing helped the habit catch on.

The sap was called *chicle* by the Mayans and *mastiche* by the Greeks, but chemists call it something different: *polyterpene*. Yep, it's a chemical, and it's a weird one. Most things you pop into your mouth and chew break up, get watered down with saliva, and break down if you swallow them. Not polyterpene. It can be rock solid at room temperature—it's only easy to chew fresh out of the package because it's mixed with sugars and other chemicals that dissolve in your mouth. Polyterpene softens at body temperature but it sticks together in a rubbery lump. Unlike butter or chocolate, it doesn't actually turn into a liquid, even if it gets really hot. And it resists all the acids in your digestive system, so if you swallow it, it stays in the same rubbery lump all the way through your body.

Weird Gum Facts

• Lots of people think that if you swallow gum, it could stay in your body for years. Most scientists disagree. It'll just come out as a rubbery lump where all the other stuff you swallowed comes out—but in very rare cases, it doesn't. It's not common, but sometimes gum gets lodged inside and forms a lump called a bezoar (see page 19) that sticks in your gut and needs to be removed surgically.

• In 1906, a fellow named Frank H. Fleer cooked up a very elastic chewing gum he called Flibber Flubber. It could stretch much farther than regular chewing gum, but he couldn't figure out how to market it. In fact, he never sold the stuff, but more than twenty years later, one of his employees tinkered with the recipe and came up with a brilliant use for it: blowing bubbles. Frank Fleer's company started selling the first bubble gum, Double Bubble, in 1928.

But just because chewing gum originally came from trees, don't think that you're popping a fruity stick of organic goodness into your mouth nowadays. The first chewing gum sold in the United States, in 1848, was John B. Curtis's State of Maine Pure Spruce Gum, but only two years later, he started selling a gum made from paraffin (wax). Sounds yucky, but it was easier to chew than spruce gum, so it was more popular. The stuff you chew now is probably made of a gummy base of styrene butadiene, polyvinyl acetate, or polyethylene.

The sapodilla's bark consists of a white, gummy latex (rubber) called *chicle*.

A Tale of Bouncy, Stretchy Chemistry

Okay, class, here's a weird chemistry question for you: What do you get when you mix the Second World War with a scientist, a toy-store owner, and a guy who needs to pay off $12,000 in debt? Give up?

You get Silly Putty, of course!

During World War II, the armed forces needed rubber for airplane and jeep tires, boots, gas masks, life vests, and more. Rubber was vital and it was in short supply. So the governments of the world issued a challenge to research scientists: create something that acts like rubber, give it to us in large amounts, and get it to us as soon as you can!

So chemists began trying to make something that acted like rubber: It had to be stretchy and easy to mold into all kinds of shapes, but solid enough to hold its shape. It had to grip onto road surfaces, but not melt when the tires warmed up. And it had to be cheap and easy to make.

In 1943, an engineer at General Electric's lab in New Haven, Connecticut, dropped two chemicals into a test tube in an attempt to make artificial rubber. James Wright was excited by the results: the boric acid and silicone oil combined into a gooey mass that bounced like rubber, stretched even better than rubber, didn't dissolve or go moldy when it got wet, and didn't melt until the temperatures got very hot. In fact, it acted a lot like rubber.

Unfortunately, it couldn't be molded into a shape—it just flattened out into a blob—so it couldn't be used to make tires or gas masks. But Wright thought that this bouncy, stretchy putty could be used for something, so he sent samples to scientists around the world. Nobody else could think of a use for it either, so Wright went back to his experimenting to help the war effort.

Over the next six years, the war ended and science marched on, but Wright's strange putty continued to circulate among scientists and their friends. Serious grown-ups would take time out to pull on it, roll it around, bounce it, and just plain play around with the stuff. They couldn't think of any practical use for it, but it was a lot of fun just to mess around with. People would even pull it out at parties for a bit of fun. In 1949, a toy-store owner named Ruth Fallgatter saw some at a party and asked an advertising man named Peter Hodgson how she could sell the stuff to her customers. Hodgson packaged it in little plastic boxes and called it Bouncing Putty. It sold pretty well, but Fallgatter thought the novelty would soon wear off so she quickly dropped the product.

Peter Hodgson saw an opportunity and seized it. He was deeply in debt and needed to raise $12,000 fast, so he took a risk. He borrowed $147 to buy a big vat full of James Wright's rubbery mixture and hundreds of red plastic Easter eggshells. He hired some college students to break off one-ounce balls of putty and stuff them into the eggshells. He gave the stuff a catchy new name, Silly Putty, and teased people with a description that didn't make sense: he called it a "real solid liquid." The combination was an instant success. This all happened more than sixty years ago, in early 1950, and Silly Putty has been popular ever since.

And people have found serious uses for it. You can stick it under the short leg of a wobbly piece of furniture. You can plug up holes with it. If you're an astronaut, you can secure tools with it in zero gravity. (The crew of Apollo 8 did!) It's also pretty good at picking up pet hair and lint and other fluffy messes. It's been used in physical therapy to build strength in injured hands, and it's also a great stress reliever—and these days, we all need something like that in our lives!

During World War II, the United States faced a shortage of natural rubber, which came from the sap (known as latex) from rubber trees. Most of the latex suppliers were Asian, and the U.S. was at war with Japan.

Where Medicines Come From

Hint: You really don't want to know! Ever since people started getting sick, we have known that certain chemicals make us feel better. In the centuries BT (before Tylenol), people would cure aches and pains by chewing willow tree bark because it contained a pain-killing chemical. They didn't know what the chemical was, but they knew it worked.

We wish all our medicines came from a source as wholesome as tree bark; however, at Weird Central, we've heard of prescriptions from sources so gross we can hardly get them past our lips to talk about them, let alone actually take them. You see, it's not just the taste of some medicines that put us off: it's where they come from.

Drink Your Mold, Dear!

Most of us have suffered from ear infections or cuts that go bad. It's a painful and rotten experience, but after a quick trip to the doctor, it's soon on the mend. That's because of a class of medicines called *antibiotics*. If you take these medicines for a few days, most infections disappear without a trace. Before antibiotics, thousands of people died from infections, so antibiotics really are miracle drugs, even if they are made from green mold! Alexander Fleming (see page 25) first discovered the germ-killing action of penicillin when he let a germ culture he was growing go moldy. He noticed that the bacteria didn't grow anywhere near the mold and started to wonder why. He extracted a liquid from green mold and discovered that it cleared up lots of different kinds of infections. Since then, many other kinds of antibiotics have been discovered and countless lives have been saved—and it all started with a dish of moldy jelly in the 1920s.

Lizard Spit for Diabetes

You've probably heard something about diabetes—it's a condition that prevents people from controlling the levels of sugar in their blood. In healthy people, an organ in the body called the *pancreas* produces a hormone called *insulin* to take care of this. Diabetics can't produce enough insulin, so they need to keep close track of what they eat and sometimes they need to take extra insulin. Of course, some of them

You can easily make your own mold. Simply place a piece of bread in a plastic bag and leave it in a dark place for a few days. After admiring your moldy bread, throw it away along with the bag. Just because it's medicine doesn't mean it's good to have around the house.

Molds, like mushrooms, are fungi. Although microscopic in size, mold grows as a connected network or colony, which you can see. Along with curing diseases, molds can also cause sicknesses such as allergies and respiratory problems. They also play an important role in biodegradation (breaking down complex materials into simpler ones), and some molds are edible, such as the mold in the blue Stilton cheese, above.

swallow poisonous lizard spit instead. A brilliant doctor from the Bronx, New York, Dr. John Eng, read somewhere that reptile venom affects the pancreas, and it got him thinking. He picked up a catalog from a reptile research lab in Utah and ordered a batch of the nastiest reptile venom he knew of: Gila monster spit. This American reptile has enough venom on its tongue to kill a human, though there have been no reported deaths from Gila monster bites since 1939.

Dr. Eng examined the venom, which contains more than a dozen different proteins and other chemicals, and found that one of them stimulated the human pancreas to produce insulin. Even better, it worked on the pancreases of people suffering from diabetes. Eventually, Dr. Eng found a way to make a synthetic version of the lizard spit, which is now prescribed under the medicinal name of Byetta.

Finish Off Your Crab!

Many of us love a crab or lobster for dinner—but nobody actually eats the shells. Or do they? People like athletes and the elderly who want to keep their joints in tip-top condition take a tablet called *glucosamine*. What they may not know is that the glucosamine they're eating comes straight from crusty crustacean shells.

Straight from the Horse's . . .

The human body creates its own chemicals to keep things rolling along smoothly. They're called *hormones*, and they control all sorts of body processes such as growth, your mood, and the levels of sugar in your blood. Sometimes, a body's hormones get out of whack and you need to take a supplement to keep them in balance. One of these is for older women and it goes under the trade name of Premarin. You know what that stands for? *Pre*gnant *mare*'s *urine*. Yep, they got mares that were expecting calves, followed them around with a bucket, and extracted the hormones from what they collected. Sound disgusting? Yep. But since it was first prescribed to women in 1942, Premarin has been a cheap and effective way to get older women's hormones in check. Don't knock it till you try it . . . but don't try it till a doctor insists!

Come and get it!

Blood Pressure Venom

In the early 1960s, a Brazilian doctor noticed something curious about snakebite victims he treated: they always fell down when they were bitten. He checked into the pit vipers that infested the banana plantations he worked for and discovered why: pit viper venom caused a big drop in blood pressure. A British doctor read about this and thought that perhaps some chemical in the venom could help patients who suffer from dangerously high blood pressure. Dr. John Vane and his colleagues used a vial of viper venom to figure out the chemical they needed to manage blood pressure better. The result was a medicine called Captopril.

The Weirdest Element

What do coal, the graphite (called "lead") in your pencil, and diamonds have in common? They're all made of exactly the same chemical: carbon. So how's that possible since one is black and crumbly, another's gray and brittle, and the third is clear and so hard it's almost indestructible? That's the beauty of carbon. It's a weird chemical, and its secret is all about how the carbon atoms hold onto each other.

In coal, carbon atoms have a loose connection with all the other carbon atoms around them. In pencil lead, the carbon holds on tight to the atoms to the right and to the left—but not so hard to the ones above and below it. And in diamonds, the carbon atoms hold on tight to all the atoms around them.

That's why coal, pencil lead, and diamonds act differently. Coal crumbles if you apply pressure to it. Pencil lead snaps if you treat it roughly, but slides off smoothly when you treat it right. When you move a pencil across a page, layers of carbon atoms slide off their upstairs neighbors but hold on tight to their next-door neighbors—that's how they draw a smooth line on the page. And in diamonds, the atoms hold on so tightly that they are very tough to break apart. In fact, diamond is one of the hardest substances on Earth. What's even weirder is that you probably have twenty pounds of carbon in your body. (A fully grown man probably has about forty-five pounds of it.)

Diamonds are hard, but like every chemical, if you get them hot enough, they'll disintegrate. With diamonds, though, you have to get it *really* hot. Diamonds evaporate at over 6,000 degrees Fahrenheit.

The Big Bang Chemicals

There's nothing we enjoy more on the Fourth of July than a good series of explosions, preferably with lots of color. And we can thank all kinds of chemicals and experiments for the fireworks we see today. In fact, it's a whole branch of science called *pyrotechnics*—the study of fire.

According to legend, it all started with an accident in a Chinese kitchen about a thousand years ago. A cook knocked a pot of flavoring onto the fire and noticed it burned in a strange way. The flavoring was a chemical called *saltpeter* (which scientists call *potassium nitrate*). When you mix it with the stuff you scrape off burned food (charcoal) and a little sulfur—all chemicals you'd find in a Chinese kitchen at the time—the black powder really flares up. This wasn't much use for cooking, but it was fun to play with. The real discovery came a few hundred years later when someone stuffed the powder into bamboo shoots and tossed it into a fire. It flared up so fast it split the bamboo open with a mighty bang. The first firecracker had been invented!

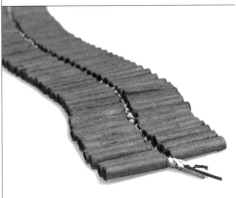

Now, nobody knows whether this is a true story or not. If it is true, the secret spread across the world to Europe by the 1200s, when the Englishman Roger Bacon wrote, "As everyone knows . . . take 7 parts of saltpeter, 5 parts of hazelwood charcoal and 5 parts of sulfur and that makes thunder and lightning." Actually, you'd need much more saltpeter to make a good explosive powder, but the basic ingredients are certainly there.

Most people call this combination *gunpowder* because it was soon used to shoot bullets and cannonballs out of weapons, but we prefer to use its

proper name, black powder, because we think the best use of it is still in fireworks. But it takes more than just black powder to make a fireworks display. There's that line in the U.S. national anthem about the rocket's red glare, but what makes black powder explode with a red flame? The answer: chemicals. A regular red comes from a lithium compound, *lithium carbonate*. A really bright red comes from *strontium carbonate*. At the right is a quick guide to the elements that make the rocket glow red, the big bang burn blue, and other explosions exhibit other colors.

Red – strontium or lithium

Orange – calcium

Yellow – sodium

White – magnesium or aluminum

Green – barium and chlorine

Blue – copper and chlorine

Purple – strontium and copper

Interview with an Explosives Expert

It's possible to grind up and mix your own chemicals to make gunpowder and use them to make your own fireworks. We know this for a fact because one of our dads used to get his saltpeter, charcoal, and sulfur by mail order to make his own when he was a kid. But he's a guy with four fingers on his left hand who doesn't answer the question, "How did you lose your pinkie, Dad?" So we suggest you leave the fireworks to the experts.

To get the score on how to make a fireworks display, we decided to talk to a real expert: Phil Grucci, whose family company makes some of the biggest pyrotechnic displays in the world. Grucci Fireworks does New Year's displays in Las Vegas, Nevada, and the enormous fireworks shows around Washington, D.C. that usher in the administration of a new president.

Weird Central: How many people do you have lighting the fuses on your larger displays?

Phil: Just one. About a quarter of our shows are fired manually from a console; the rest are done automatically by a computer. We use electronic fuses; the electricity is carried along phone lines. This lets us do things we could never do by hand. Let's say we have a single item that fires twenty-five feet in the air and explodes in a pattern that lasts about a second. It looks pretty good, but if you take a hundred of them and fire them off six ledges on Rockefeller Center, and time it so all one hundred of them fire off a tenth of a second apart . . . the effect is much more dramatic! You need a computer system for that and some refined pyrotechnics.

WC: So a pyrotechnic display is one part computer science and one part chemistry?

Phil: It's many things. With our Golden Flitter Split Comet, for example, thirty-five separate comet fireworks are launched in a shell. It's a cardboard cylinder with stages in it, separated by cardboard disks. And there's a fuse running through the middle of each disk. When the shell reaches a certain height, the comets ignite, break out of the shell, and form a pattern like a spider. Then they explode and split again.

There's a lot going on there. The gold color and how it burns a twinkling gold, that's down to chemistry. (Mixed in with the black powder, you have aluminum for sparkle and compounds containing antimony and sodium for color). The splitting is all engineering. There's a burst charge in each comet that bursts it open a second time. The whole thing is a combination of chemistry, physics, engineering, and art.

WC: Did you say "art"?

Phil: Oh, yes. Pyrotechnics is considered an art form. The product is manufactured by hand; it's crafted. The design is based on the senses: you see and hear fireworks, you can smell them, you can sometimes even feel the reverberations. We are designers who work with a cast of characters (the fireworks), and we choreograph the cast. What comes first is the event—say, a Fourth of July show. What's the need? To celebrate our independence. What is the theme of the program? It's patriotic. The second is the selection of the musical score. When you have the music, you look at the stage you're working from. Sometimes it's a barge in the middle of a river or the rooftop of a hotel or just an open field . . . that's your stage. I'm selecting the characters and scripting when they appear on the stage. Sometimes the choice is easy. If you have someone singing "God Bless the USA," we could have shells spell out the letters U S A. Sometimes, the effects we use are more subtle.

WC: How long does it take to get a fifteen-minute or half-hour firework display together?

Phil: The scripting takes about one hour per minute of fireworks that you see. . . . But a lot has to happen before we can start scripting. It normally takes two or three months of preparation, at least. For [large shows], we work virtually all year long. You can still smell the smoke from this year's display when we start thinking about next year's.

Soda Fountains

You've probably seen or heard about what happens when you drop a few mints into a bottle of diet cola. It's not quite like a firework, but the explosive gushing of fizzy liquid isn't far off, and some crazy folks have made amazing displays of it. We're thinking of two guys in white coats and red ties. They call themselves EepyBird, but their actual names are Fritz Grobe and Stephen Voltz. They're the guys in the famous online videos who make fountains of soda gush out in amazing patterns. They've also made a car propelled entirely by the reaction you get when you drop Mentos mints into two-liter bottles of Diet Coke.

But what's going on in these experiments? Well, it took scientists a while to figure it out. First, you need to know what soda is made of. It's basically water with several chemicals dissolved in it. Soda contains flavoring, coloring, and sugar or some other chemical to make it sweet, but the fizz is caused by dissolving lots of gas into the mixture. The gas in question, carbon dioxide, is the one that animals breathe out and that plants breathe in. It's made up of one carbon atom and two oxygen atoms. When you dissolve it in water, you make a mild acid called *carbonic acid*. But carbon dioxide doesn't like to stay dissolved. That's why it jumps out of the solution in the form of bubbles.

Lots of things make gas bubble out of soda. Taking the cap off a bottle releases pressure, which makes it fizz up. Shaking the bottle first just makes the gas want to jump out faster. And putting something into the soda that changes the chemistry of the liquid can also force out carbon dioxide. Some scientists, including the *Mythbusters* TV stars, suggested that the Mentos and Diet Coke effect might be a chemical reaction: there's gum arabic and gelatin in the candy and caffeine, benzoate, and aspartame in the soda. However, according to the

Fritz Grobe and Stephen Voltz—
the mad scientists behind EepyBird.

American Journal of Physics, a team of scientists at Appalachian State University in Boone, North Carolina, found the real cause. Putting soda in contact with a rough surface really brings the gas out. Pour soda on a kitchen counter and bubbles will come out quite quickly. (And so will your mom to tell you to mop it up!) That's because a countertop is rougher than the inside of a glass. Pour soda on the sidewalk, and the bubbles will come up really fast because sidewalks are really rough. It turns out that Mentos mints have a very rough surface as well. Millions of tiny bubbles of carbon dioxide jump out of the soda onto the surface of the mint and then float up to the surface. That's what causes the gushing fountains of soda when you drop in a bunch of Mentos.

EepyBird launched this cola-and-mint-propelled vehicle 221 feet using 108 bottles of Coke Zero and 648 Mentos. You can watch this and other extreme experiments at www.eepybird.com.

Want to Try This at Home?

What You Need

- EepyBird recommends using a warm (80 to 90 degrees Fahrenheit) two-liter bottle of Diet Coke or Coke Zero (if you use regular cola instead of diet, you'll get a sticky, syrupy mess everywhere)
- Four to six Mentos (you can also try other mints)
- A piece of paper
- Tape
- A playing card or another thin piece of cardboard
- A wide-open outdoor space
- Your parents' permission

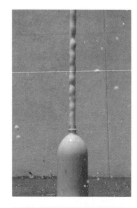

What You Do

1. Find an outdoor location where it's okay to make a mess. (And promise to clean up afterward.)

2. Roll a piece of paper into a tube that the mints will fit in and tape the tube together.

3. Place the mints in the tube and the thin piece of cardboar underneath one of the tube openings.

4. Open the diet cola and place the cardboard over the open cola bottle.

5. When you're ready to launch, hold the tube and quickly pull the card out from underneath.

6. Run like crazy . . . and enjoy the show.

I studied gases.

Soda Scientists

Do you have any idea who invented soda? No, it wasn't Dr. Pepper or Mr. Pibb. It was an Englishman named Joseph Priestley, a friend of Benjamin Franklin's. Priestley studied gases and made many important discoveries in the late eighteenth century. He collected the gas given off during the process of brewing beer, and he found that animals couldn't breathe it and fire wouldn't burn in it. This obviously meant that the atmosphere contained different gases, and with experimentation, he isolated two of them: the breathable gas, which we now call oxygen, and the nonbreathable gas, which he called fixed air—carbon dioxide. He noticed that *fixed air* easily dissolved in water, making a drink with "peculiar spirit and virtues." We like it, too! But we're not so sure about the name he used for oxygen: he called it *dephlogisticated* air.

MYSTERIOUS PHENOMENA

Science is all about solving mysteries. Everything we know about the world around us started out with some scientist looking at clues like a detective would, thinking, testing out theories, and figuring out the real story. That's why science is so important. But there are still many mysteries in the world, and at Weird Central, we enjoy collecting them and wondering what they're about.

Our favorite researcher from the past hundred years or so was a man named Charles Hoy Fort. He spent most of his working life in libraries collecting strange stories from newspapers and publishing them in books. He always challenged scientists to explain what he found, and most of the time they couldn't. That's why we like Fort so much: he didn't ignore evidence just because it wasn't easy to explain.

One word many weird watchers love to use is *phenomenon*. A phenomenon could be any event you can observe, but usually it means a really strange one. You wouldn't call a rainstorm a phenomenon, but if it the raindrops were inky black or red, you would! (Yes, that's actually happened, as you'll see in this chapter). So let's look at some mysterious phenomena and see if we can come up with some explanations.

Stormy Weather

Did you ever notice how often people talk about the weather? We here at Weird Central think it's strange. There are only a few kinds of weather—it's all made up of some combination of hot, cold, wet, cloudy, misty, sunny, rainy, humid, windy, and snowy. But still people ask, "How about this weather?" We like to throw a little weirdness into our replies. "It could be worse . . . it could be raining frogs . . . or hair . . . or fish!" And it has happened before! Here are just a few freakish rainfalls we've found in our files.

Fish Storm

In 1947, in Marksville, Louisiana, a biologist from the Louisiana Department of Wildlife and Fisheries experienced a rainstorm like nothing he'd ever seen before. As he walked down Main Street, hundreds of fish fell from the sky, hitting pedestrians and cars. As an expert in local animals, he recognized they were native to the area. But how did they get up into the clouds? He didn't know.

Almost forty years later, a fishing boat on Lake Michigan had a similar problem. There was a heavy storm, the boat's engines failed, and as the crew struggled to keep the boat afloat, thousands of tiny fish

Charles Fort (1874–1932) was a writer and researcher who collected thousands of stories of odd phenomena—occurrences that couldn't be explained by science or that were considered beyond what scientists would consider "acceptable." His collection included true stories of teleportation, poltergeists, raining frogs and fish, spontaneous combustion, levitation, UFOs, giant wheels of light in oceans, strange items found in unlikely locations, and alien abductions. These phenomena are often referred to as *Forteana*, in honor of Charles Fort. Many researchers and scientists have since sought to disprove Fort's bizarre stories; however, as Fort himself wrote, "I offer the data. Suit yourself."

(called smelts) pelted down in the rain. There were so many of them, the trawler almost capsized! One possible explanation: strong storms could whip up spouts of water from lakes or seas and toss them—and the fish inside them—across great distances.

Meat Storm

Feeling hungry? Well, you could always eat whatever the rain brought down. In Kentucky in 1876, chunks of meat rained down. Two men tasted the three-inch cubes of meat and said they tasted like beef or venison. They regretted it later, when someone observed that there had been a huge group of buzzards flying over the town and suggested that the birds may have thrown up the meat.

Bat Storm

A rainstorm in Fort Worth, Texas, in 1989 sent residents screaming for cover. It wasn't just the heavy thudding sound of the raindrops that did it, but the hundreds of sick bats making an even louder thud as they struck cars, umbrellas, and trees on their way down.

Frog Storm

In 1891, a freak storm in Bournemouth, England, littered the countryside with yellow frogs. Regular greenish frogs have also fallen in France (in 1794 and 1833, in the towns of Lelain and Versailles), and northern Greece in 1963 and 1979. So many frogs fell in Greece in 1979 that traffic couldn't move through the towns!

Hair Storm

In October 1959, thousands of strands of silver hair fell on Savannah, Georgia, covering trees and houses. Almost exactly ten years later, in October 1969, hundreds of calls came into police stations and news services in St. Louis, Missouri, reporting similar fine filaments of hair raining down on the town. Though these cases are still unsolved, some insect experts believe that they were bits of web that young spiders spin as a kind of parachute to help them fly away from home.

Mud Storm

During a January 1998 evening, Rose Snell returned to her home in Paradise Township, Pennsylvania, to find mud splattered across her door. She thought it was a prank played by kids, but when she looked around, she saw it was all over one side of her house and the nearby trees. All of the other houses in the neighborhood were clean. We can only guess that a freak mud shower passed through and hit only her house, but we can't tell for sure.

Worm Storm

A newspaper in Palmyra, Wisconsin, ran this odd headline in April 1897: "A Shower of Worms!" How weird is that? According to the article, the creepy crawlers were everywhere—strewn across the ground, oozing out of buckets. Ewww! Fortunately, they quickly wiggled into the earth where they belonged. No airborne worms have been reported since then. But eagle-eyed researchers found out that something similar had happened in 1872 in Romania, when a single rain cloud had deposited enough black worms to coat the streets of the city of Bucharest.

Scientists seeking to explain these weird, well-documented "falls" say that tornadoes or waterspouts can lift animals and other objects into the air and deposit them miles away.

How about a couple of these fellas falling on your head?

UF "O"s

You've probably seen some amazing photographs of strange patterns in cornfields or wheat fields. You can only clearly see these patterns, called *crop circles*, from the air, and they look spectacular. Most people dismiss them as pranks or art projects, and some of them are. Back in 1991, Doug Bower and Dave Chorley explained how they had been making patterns in crops since 1978. They showed how with planks, blueprints, and string, they could make dozens of different patterns quite quickly. But does that mean the case is closed? We don't think so.

Some crop circles aren't that attractive to look at. They're hardly the finely made geometric shapes that Doug and Dave made. Many people feel sick and fatigued when they stand near these sloppy crop circles. Their hair stands on end and their camera batteries drain quickly in the area. Eyewitnesses see lights or hear buzzing sounds in areas where crop circles appear. Nothing in Doug and Dave's projects could explain that. And besides, crop circles began long before these two started their work.

That's why researchers look into these circles very carefully. They apply scientific methods to analyze the sites and samples of broken cornstalks. And some of their findings are fascinating! We caught up with a field researcher who works with the BLT Group (named for the initials of its three founders, John Burke, Dr. W. C. Leavengood, and Nancy Talbott). We interviewed George Reynolds, a retired army systems engineer and an expert in instrumentation. He told us quite a tale of field research in . . . well . . . fields. (Read the interview on the next page.)

This crop circle appeared in a field in Milk Hill, England, in 2001. It was 780 feet in diameter and was composed of 409 circles.

A crop circle in Switzerland.

George Reynolds: Crop circles are real, but crop circles are being forged all the time. You do get fakes—I've made my own. There are several ways you can tell a real crop circle from a "Doug-and-Dave." When you take it apart, you find that it's not just tramped down, it's down in three or four different levels; one layer's going east to west, one's on top of it going to the south—it's not lying down like somebody's tramped it. When you take a stalk of wheat or rye or oats from inside a circle, you find thick rings around the stem. We call them nodules. The top ring is bent and it's exploded. It's literally blown up. It's like you're looking at the moon with all the cavities in it. Throw a stalk in the microwave for thirty seconds and it'll pop the same way. There's three times as much water in the nodule as there is in the stem. Sometimes some of the other nodules will get it, too, but the top one's the one that gets the worst bending.

WC: How do you analyze a crop circle properly?

GR: You take crop samples, one foot out, two feet out, four, sixteen, a hundred, in different directions. Then you take soil samples and send them to a lab for analysis. I take magnetometers to look at the magnetic fields, and I take electrostatic meters and radioactivity detectors. You take many, many photographs. I've got a radar detector in my car, and I got within an eighth of a mile of one crop circle site and the radar detector started to talk to me: it was going, "Whop, whop, whop." The next day, I took the radar detector and hooked it up to a 12-volt battery and took it around this place, and everywhere I went, the thing was going, "Whop, whop, whop."

WC: What kind of activity could cause that kind of damage to crops?

GR: We don't know. Most people think it's some kind of an energy that comes down from above.

WC: What's it like being in the middle of a crop circle?

GR: There are no insects, no birds, nothing. I had some guy come from the city with his camera, and I told him not to step in the circle, because people had trouble with their batteries. He said, "No, I just charged it last night." He steps in, and his camera's red light comes on . . . the battery's dead. So he put the second set in . . . he wouldn't listen to me; he knew everything (he's a smart guy from the city). He stepped inside, and the second battery died on him. That's the kind of thing that happens. I started doing an investigation into magnetic fields. I laid a compass into the crop circle and the compass started to swing like the pendulum of a clock. Then it started rotating like a motor. I'd never seen anything like it.

WC: This is a fringe field for a scientist to be working in. Do people outside of the world of crop circles treat you with respect?

GR: I get a lot of lip, but I've learned a lot. You don't argue. If a guy doesn't believe in crop circles, I'll say that's your opinion, I got mine, let's talk about something else.

Spontaneous Human Combustion

If there's one thing that we remember from camping trips with the Scouts, it's that you can't set fire to wet stuff. But there's evidence that something that's more than 50 percent water not only burns, but bursts into flame for no reason. Want to know something even freakier? The thing in question is the human body. Yep, for about two hundred years, there have been cases of burned bodies that firefighters and scientists can't account for. It looks like the fires that killed these poor souls started inside their own bodies. They call this phenomenon *spontaneous human combustion*, or SHC. That's a lot of syllables that mean one thing: people bursting into flames for no good reason. It's creepy to think about, but it's also fascinating, because a healthy human body is 57 percent water. Even if you're unhealthily obese or dehydrated, you're still about 45 percent water. That's a lot of water to put out a fire! But spontaneous human combustion still takes place—or so people think. Check out these famous cases and see if you can come up with an explanation.

Allen M. Small, Deer Isle, Maine, January 1943

Police discovered Mr. Small's body as they entered his home. His body was charred and the burned carpet underneath showed that fifty-two-year-old Mr. Small had died in a fire. But the police couldn't understand how the fire had started and why nothing else in the room caught fire. From the evidence, it almost seemed as though the source of the fire was the victim, Mr. Small.

Mary Reeser, St. Petersburg, Florida, July 1951

By the time firemen extinguished the blaze, all that was left of sixty-seven-year-old Mary Reeser was her skull, one slipper-covered foot, and a pile of ashes. Experts estimated that the room had reached a temperature of 3,000 degrees Fahrenheit, but the heat damage was minimal. And there was no fire damage outside of the four-foot area where Mrs. Reeser had been sitting. "Unusual and improbable" was the conclusion in the official report. Sounds like SHC to us!

Helen Conway, Upper Darby Township, Pennsylvania, November 1964

Ecch! Blech! To be honest, this one is almost too much for our poor, weak stomachs. We'll spare you the grisly details but simply mention that this case is very similar to that of Mary Reeser, except, instead of a foot, the firemen found two legs, which were intact from the knees down and propped up against a chair (indicating that Mrs. Conway had been sitting when the "event" occurred). Even the fire chief, Paul Haggarty, was convinced that Mrs. Conway had spontaneously combusted.

Looking for Mary Reeser . . . or what's left of her.

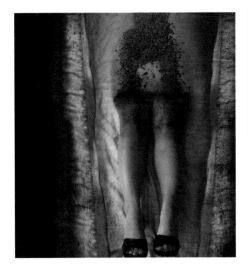

From the Evergreen State comes this uncanny story of an exploding corpse. Here are the facts: The fire broke out in the Coleman Funeral Home. At the center of the inferno was a coffin containing the remains of Betty Satlow. When the firefighters arrived, the doors to the funeral home were still locked. No signs of a break-in. No evidence of an accelerant such as gasoline or lighter fluid. No explanation besides the nagging possibility that this was an odd instance of spontaneous human combustion. Or, dare we say it . . . spontaneous human cremation?

The World's Slowest Racetrack

California's Death Valley is a creepy kind of place that looks like another world. But if the Martian terrain isn't enough to jangle your nerves, how about the weird rocks of the Racetrack Playa? About thirty miles away from the Ubehebe volcanic crater at the north end of the valley is the dried bed of what was once an ancient lake. Off in the distance you can see blurry black dots on the horizon. They are dark boulders that move, either when people aren't looking, or so slowly, you can't see the movement. But each of them has a trail after it, as if it's been crawling along that lake bed for hundreds of years.

Some trails are perfectly straight, many others zigzag around, and some even turn back on themselves. It's weird and exhilarating at the same time. Many of the rocks have even pushed up a lip of dried mud in front of them. And only a very few appear to have moved in the same direction. There are no footprints or tire tracks to hint that humans moved the rocks. It's almost as if they were ALIVE! They're not, of course, but what else explains the fact that they really do move? The cracked, dry floor of the valley is flat. The wind couldn't push a rock across a dry, dusty plain—and even if it could, would it push the rocks in the zigzag pattern of the trails behind these rocks?

Death Valley, California.

And here's an even bigger question: How did these rocks travel so far from the mountains they broke away from? These unanswerable questions, along with the unearthly beauty of Death Valley, make Racetrack Playa one of the must-see destinations in Weird America. When you go, weigh the idea that some scientists have put forward to explain this phenomenon: ice forms under the boulders, which makes the path slick enough for a strong wind to blow them. We don't know . . . does that sound realistic to you?

Lights in the Sky

There are many legends from around the world of strange lights luring people into trouble by night. The most famous are the marsh lights called *will-o'-the-wisp*, which scientists now believe are caused by puffs of inflammable gas flaring up as they seep out of bogs. Because people in the old days thought the lights were from people carrying candles, many nighttime hikers got their boots wet following lights into the marshes! But there are other strange lights that show up in specific places in the United States that are a bit more mysterious.

The Ghost Lights of West Texas

Back in the 1880s, the area around Marfa, Texas, was sparsely populated with a few homesteaders in cabins. One of the pioneers, Robert Ellison, was frightened one night by the sight of campfires out in the wilderness. He was afraid that Apaches were getting ready to attack him. But as he looked more closely at the lights, he saw something strange—the lights weren't still at all. They bobbed around and floated and bounced through the scrubland. It wasn't possible to explain how a human could make light move that way. If the Marfa lights had come and gone like so many strange phenomena, the story may well have ended before the nineteenth century. But as the area became built up, the lights kept showing up. They still do. To see them for yourself, travel east from Marfa on US 90 until you get to the Marfa's Mystery Lights Viewing Area—yes, Marfa is proud of their strange phenomenon and wants everyone to come take a look. From here, most people can see strange white lights on the horizon, appearing one at a time and then fading away quickly. Though they are miles off in the distance, they're easy to see. But they're hard to explain. One explanation is what scientists call *tunneling refraction*. You know the mirage effect—where sunlight on a distant highway looks like a pool of water? And when you drive closer to it, the water disappears? Tunneling refraction is like a very complicated version of the same thing. The idea is that light from somewhere refracts across the empty plains and appears in the air instead of on a road. But what gives off enough light at night to create these rocking, bouncing lights? The moon? The stars? Who knows? Your guess is as good as ours.

Long Valley Lights—Home of the Hookerman

The great thing about mysteries is that people love coming up with explanations. And the strange bouncing lights around New Jersey's Long Valley, known as the "Hookerman lights," gave birth to one of the more outlandish explanations we've heard: It was the ghost of a railway worker who lost his arm back in the 1800s and had a hook to replace it. Now that he's dead, he wanders around the site of the old railroad looking for his arm with a ghostly light. Thrill seekers by the hundreds have been out to look for his ghostly swinging light—and they've seen it. But what they've actually seen is something a bit more thrilling: a bright amber-colored light, shaped like a ball or disk, about four feet across. It moves about ten to twelve feet above the tracks at twenty-five to forty miles per hour.

In 1976, a group of investigators took a Geiger counter, methane detectors, and four thousand feet of copper attached to oscilloscopes and went out to the tracks to see what they could find. At 10:00 PM on November 20, the light appeared a foot above the ground, hovered there for about two minutes, and vanished. Their instruments registered all kinds of electromagnetic activity but no radiation or marsh gases. We received a note from Anthony Muller, a science teacher in Mt. Arlington, New Jersey, who has spent a lot of time studying the Hookerman lights, and he wrote, "I was quite interested in this phenomenon and began some research. Geologists and electrical engineers told me that quartz-bearing rocks, under pressure and stress, produce electrical discharges in what is known as the *piezoelectric effect*. The railroad tracks may focus this electrical energy into ball lightning or something close to it."

Wow! Ball lightning! In this case, the scientific explanation is almost as weird as the spooky folk legend.

Hookerman Crossing.

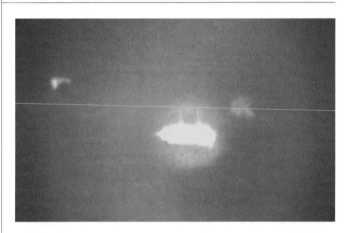

The Hookerman lights in action!

Solving Mysteries

So how can science help figure out these mysteries? Well, let's take an example from history and see what evidence we can put together. Back in the year 535 CE, a series of strange phenomena took place. Looking at the evidence, it's hard to figure out what might have caused them. Take a look at these clues and see if you can figure it out.

CLUE 1: In the year 535, provinces throughout southern China heard a series of loud bangs from the south. Reports of it appear in court records of the time. This happened before the invention of gunpowder, so it wasn't bombs or guns. And it wasn't thunder either since nobody would bother to write about a distant thunderstorm in an important court record. So these bangs were obviously something strange . . . but what?

CLUE 2: Legends around the world tell of the skies and the moon turning to blood—or at least turning bloodred. Many people saw these legends as bad omens, signs of terrible things to come. But are these stories legends or are they somehow connected with the explosive noises?

CLUE 3: The next clue comes from almost three thousand miles south of southern China, on the island of Java—and it's a bit more subtle. The kings of Java used to keep a journal of events on the island written on palm leaves. There would be at least two records per year, and they still exist. But there are no records at all for eighteen years after the explosions were heard in China. What could have caused a nation of record keepers to just stop for almost two decades?

CLUE 4: Another clue came from New Zealand, almost five thousand miles away from Java. Every year a tree grows, it adds a ring to its trunk. If you cut into a tree trunk, you can tell how old it is by counting the rings. You can also tell by the size of the rings how much growing a tree did that year. Counting back through the rings of old trees, science detectives noticed the tree rings were very thin in the years following the loud bangs.

What made the moon turn red more than 1,500 years ago?

Dendochronology is the method of dating using tree rings. With it, scientists can date the time when tree rings were formed—sometimes to the exact calendar year. A tiny ring could mean a year with little rain or sunshine.

CLUE 5: On the polar ice caps, layers of ice gather every year. By cutting deep into the old ice, scientists can get samples that tell us about what was floating in the air at any time in history. Around the time of the loud bangs, there was a gray-black dust in the air.

These five clues don't give us much to go on. Were they all connected somehow? If so, how? Can you guess what might have caused these phenomena? Well, it took scientists more than a thousand years to figure out exactly what happened—and they were only sure after they saw a repeat of the same event and collected many of the same results. So, what happened?

The Bang That Was Heard around the World

In the summer of 1883, ships carrying coffee and spices to Europe from the Indonesian island of Java saw a huge cloud of white smoke coming out of the tiny island of Krakatoa. Using their ship's instruments, they calculated that the huge plumes of smoke reached seven miles high. There was a thunderous noise in the air, like cannons firing, with a crackling noise underneath it. And there were fiery lights like lightning in the clouds. This was a busy shipping route, so many people saw this and reported that their ships were covered with a sticky gray dust. The air was so bad that people were gasping for breath. And then the island exploded.

The eruption of the volcanic island of Krakatoa happened when science and technology were getting quite advanced. This happened in the days before telephones, but a recent invention called the telegraph (which was a kind of old-fashioned Internet) let news of Krakatoa travel around the world in a matter of hours—so scientists could analyze the eruption. Scientists from the Royal Society in England decided they would collect as much data as they could about the event, so that the world could spot all the symptoms of a big volcanic eruption. Their findings were amazing.

The sound of Krakatoa exploding was so loud that ships and towns and army bases for thousands of miles around, as far away as Australia and China, went on red alert—they thought they were being attacked! To get some idea of the scale here: it would be like a loud noise in New York being heard as far away as London and Los Angeles.

The dirt and dust from the explosion got into the upper atmosphere and went all around the world. In the weeks that followed, ash fell in rain as far away as America and Europe. The dust in the sky made for weirdly colorful sunsets where the moon seemed blue, green, or bloodred. It's too bad that color photography wasn't around in those days! The only photos we have are black and white. Weather stations across Europe at the time used barometers to check changes in air pressure, which helped them predict weather. In the days after the explosion of Krakatoa, the air pressure changed in weird ways. When the Royal Society looked at the timing of these changes, they realized what had happened: The changes in air pressure were caused by shock waves from Krakatoa! They spread across the world in a big wave—then met at the opposite end of the world and echoed back across the world. When the shock waves got back to Java, they echoed again! In all, the exploding volcano sent shock waves around the world seven times.

All this shed some light on the strange phenomena from 535 CE, mentioned earlier. The bangs back in ancient history were obviously the eruption of an explosive volcano like Krakatoa. Volcanoes like this send up dust that darkens the skies for thousands of miles around—robbing plants of sunlight and making them grow slowly and dropping dust on countries thousands of miles away. And as for the eighteen-year gap in Java's palm-leaf records—well, a huge, explosive volcano must have made Java into a disaster area. It could have taken many years to recover from that, so perhaps instead of writing about the events, the people were rebuilding their civilization.

So we can see that not every mystery remains one forever. Perhaps soon we will have an explanation of all the mysteries in this chapter. But for now it's kind of fun to read and talk about them while we scratch our heads.

ILLOGICAL LEAPS

In their quest for knowledge, scientists often follow up on weird hunches. They propose preposterous theories and conduct strange studies. Most often their efforts lead nowhere, but sometimes the results are groundbreaking. To illustrate, we'll tell you the tale of Karl Ritter von Frisch and his waggle-dancing bees.

Von Frisch (1886–1982) was an Austrian scientist who studied honeybees. In the 1920s, he announced his theory that honeybees do a waggle dance to tell other bees where to find flowers. Von Frisch even claimed to have translated the busy buzzing and whirling bee movements, unlocking the secrets of the mysterious waggle dance. At the time, scientists were skeptical and rejected von Frisch's farfetched theory that bees had a language of their own (and one that we could actually come to understand). Soon enough, von Frisch's analysis of the waggle dance was proven to be correct and, in 1973, the scientist was awarded the Nobel Prize. In this chapter, you'll read about scientists who ask crazy questions such as, "Why don't woodpeckers get headaches?" and "Is Kansas really as flat as a pancake?" You'll wonder how anyone could take this stuff seriously. In many instances, you'll be right to scoff—some of the experiments presented here are undeniably silly! But keep in mind those waggle-dancing bees. Perhaps some of these leaps aren't so illogical after all.

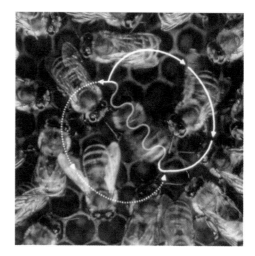

The waggle-dance diagram.

And the Ig Nobel Prize Goes to . . .

The highest honor a scientist can obtain is the Nobel Prize. Started in 1901, the awards are named after Swedish chemist Alfred Nobel, the man who invented dynamite. Feeling terrible about the destruction that his creation had caused, Nobel proposed an award for high achievements that benefit mankind.

The Ig Nobel Prizes are something else entirely. The word *ignoble* means "low-minded and crude" and, true to its name, the Ig Nobel Prize is a celebration of low (or possibly questionable) achievement in science and other fields. The prizes are awarded by a magazine called the *Annals of Improbable Research*. According to its founders, "Improbable research is research that makes people laugh and then think." The Ig Nobels elicit more giggles than deep thought but the prizewinners are an impressive bunch. In fact, Dutch scientist Andre Geim has been awarded both a Nobel and an Ig Nobel. (In 2000, he won an Ig for levitating a frog with magnets. His Nobel Prize in 2010 was for something considerably less silly.)

Do scientists view the booby prize as an insult? Not at all! They're usually good-humored about the honor and even take it as a compliment. Often wearing funny costumes, they come to the annual Ig Nobel ceremony where they pick up their award and give a little acceptance speech. Here are some recent recipients of the great and goofy Ig.

2009 Ig Nobel Prize for Medicine, Donald Unger of Thousand Oaks, California

As a boy, Donald's mother scolded him for cracking his knuckles, insisting that the habit would lead to arthritis, a disease affecting the joints of the body. Inspired by her pestering, the scientifically minded boy started a knuckle-cracking experiment. Twice each day, he made sure to crack his knuckles, but only those on his left hand. The knuckles of his right hand were off limits. As best as he could, he always carefully avoided cracking them. This went on for fifty years and finally led to an article called "Does Knuckle Cracking Lead to Arthritis of the Fingers?" In this paper, Unger revealed that, after five decades of left-hand-only knuckle cracking, there was no difference between the knuckles on his left and right hands. When he accepted his Ig Nobel Prize in 2009, he raised his hands and jokingly cried out to the heavens. "Mother, I know you can hear me. Mother, you were wrong! And now that I have your attention, can I stop eating my broccoli, please?"

Maybe my dynamite invention should have received an Ig Nobel Prize.

So, what are you waiting for? Get cracking!

2009 Ig Nobel Prize for Physics, Katherine K. Whitcome of Cincinnati, Ohio

Along with two other scientists, Dr. Whitcome studied pregnant women to see why they don't tip over. The reason: women have an extra-curvy spine that helps them lean backward and carry the extra weight. You know what this means? Men with big bellies are more inclined to topple. Watch out!

No worries here!

2006 Ig Nobel Prize for Ornithology, Ivan R. Schwab and Philip R. A. May of California

Schwab and May finally answered the nagging question: Why don't woodpeckers get headaches, brain damage, or eye injuries? (Uh, the answer's complicated, but it seems that they have elastic bones and strong neck muscles to help cushion the blows, and they have a thick, extra eyelid to keep their eyes from popping out.) Ivan Schwab, an eye doctor (or ophthalmologist) accepted his prize wearing a woodpecker hat with a red, fluffy, feathery top and a long, pointy beak.

2006 Ig Nobel Prize for Acoustics, D. Lynn Halpern of Massachusetts, Randolph Blake and James Hillenbrand of Illinois

The team of scientists struggled to determine exactly why the sound of fingernails on a blackboard is unpleasant. At the Ig Nobel ceremony, Halpern and Blake rolled out a blackboard and proceeded to make the audience squirm. *Screeeech!*

2001 Ig Nobel Prize for Biology, Buck Weimer of Pueblo, Colorado

Chester "Buck" Weimer won his Ig for inventing Under-Ease: airtight underwear specially designed to filter out "bad-smelling gases." His company, UnderTec, has a motto that says it all: "Wear them for the ones you love."

Got aspirin?

Mirthful Machines

In medicine, robots help doctors perform complicated surgical maneuvers. In space, robots allow scientists to remotely explore the surfaces of distant planets. However, there are some areas where robots are virtually useless. Take comedy, for example. Robots can't laugh, and even if they could, they wouldn't know *when* to laugh. This probably doesn't sound like a big deal, but imagine a future where you interacted with robots on a daily basis. Would you want to be surrounded by straight-faced robots that never cracked a smile? Of course not!

Fortunately, a team of scientists at the Signal Analysis Interpretation Laboratory (SAIL) in California is trying to bridge the gap between robots and comedy. Led by Professor Shrikanth S. Narayanan, they are working on a "Synthetic Laughter Generator," which might someday enable robots to emit convincing giggle noises. (Recently, we heard a little sample and it sounded like . . . a robot chuckling! What else would you expect?)

Once SAIL irons out the kinks, robots and other machines will start laughing. But how will they know when to laugh? SAIL scientists are hoping to crack this challenge as well. In addition to the "Synthetic Laughter Generator," laboratory scientists are developing a technology for "sarcasm recognition." Just in case you're not familiar with sarcasm, we'll fill you in. If you say something and you obviously mean the opposite, you're being sarcastic. For example, if you meet a Flat Earther who insists that the Earth is shaped like a poker chip (see page 103), you might say, "Yeah, right!" when of course you mean, "You're wrong!" That's sarcasm!

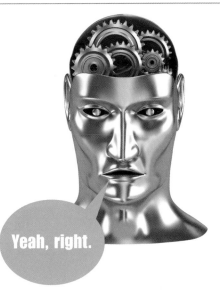

SAIL scientists listened to recorded phone conversations and noted every time they heard someone say, "Yeah, right!" Each time they encountered the phrase, they measured the amount of sarcasm used, and with this information, they taught computers how to recognize sarcastic speech patterns.

What's next for the scientists at SAIL? Synthetically generated knock-knock jokes? Sad-faced robot clowns? Remote-controlled stand-up comics? The possibilities are endless. (Yeah, right!)

The White Bear Experiment

In 1987, psychology professor Daniel Wegner gave the following strange instructions to students participating in a study:

1. Sit in a room and speak about whatever pops into your mind.

2. Try not to think about a white bear.

3. If you slip up and think about a white bear or if you say the words "white bear," ring a bell.

You can probably guess the results. Ding! Ding! Ding! The students thought about white bears even though they were instructed not to. Other scientists wondered if they'd get the same results if they used an imaginary animal instead of a white bear, so they conducted a "green rabbit" experiment. This time, the participants had green rabbits on the brain.

Of course, this research had nothing to do with white bears or green rabbits. It was about thought suppression. In other words, the scientists were interested in exploring what happens when we try not to think about something.

Daniel Wegner's weird "white bear" experiment is now considered a classic psychology study. It suggests that the more we try to control our own thoughts, the more we fail. If we try to forget sweets, we have candy bars dancing in our heads. If we're ordered not to be afraid, we just grow more frightened. And if we're asked not to think about white bears, we become obsessed with them.

Don't believe us? Give it a try. Right now, try not to think of a white bear. Go ahead and stop thinking about white bears! (Good luck with that.)

Tickle Torture

Didn't we tell you to stop thinking about white bears?

To help rid your mind of those unwanted cuddly cubs, we'll distract you with a couple of experiments delving into the mysterious phenomenon of *gargalesis*, better known as tickling. Not to be confused with *knismesis* (which is light, feather, kitchy-kitchy-koo tickling), gargalesis is heavy, laughter-provoking, no-please-stop-please-please-stop tickling.

In 1933, Ohio psychology professor Clarence Leuba decided to study the subject by tickling his own son. With his research, he was hoping to answer the question: Are children taught to laugh when they're tickled or do they laugh because they can't help it?

To conduct his experiment, he established a few rules. No tickling would occur at the Leuba house except during specially designated tickle periods. During these tickling sessions, no adults were allowed to smile. To make sure that Leuba himself wasn't caught smiling, the scientist wore a mask whenever he tickled his son.

The boy was tickled regularly and with scientific precision. First, under the arm. Next, under the ribs. Then the chin. The neck. *Whoooo! Whahahahahahaaaah!*

Aside from one mess-up by Leuba's wife (she accidentally tickled her son after giving him a bath), the experiment proceeded as planned. Finally, after tickling his son, and then his daughter, for years, Leuba reached a conclusion: we laugh when we're being tickled for the same reason we say, "Achoo!" when we sneeze—it's natural!

Another gargantuan moment in gargalesis research came about sixty years later. In a 1999 paper entitled "Can a Machine Tickle?" Dr. Christine Harris described a study she'd conducted at the University of California psychology lab.

In the experiment, Dr. Harris led participants into a room and, showed them a vibrating gizmo with a mechanical hand. She told them this crazy device was a tickle machine. The subjects were then blindfolded and, with their bare feet on a stool, they were tickled. (Actually, researchers did all the foot tickling. The tickle machine didn't really work. It was just a believable fake.)

Dr. Harris had concocted this scenario because she wondered if tickling was a social activity, something people did together like

Scientists have proven that tickling someone's feet eventually leads to getting kicked in the head.

chess or Ping-Pong. She was curious if ticklish people would still be ticklish if they were convinced that a robot was tickling them.

Do you think you'd giggle if you thought you were being tickled by a tickle machine? If you're as ticklish as we are, you probably answered, "Yes!" And that's exactly what Dr. Harris discovered. Her test subjects hooted and hollered, laughed and giggled uncontrollably, even though they believed that their feet were being touched by a machine. This result implies that tickling doesn't require other people. It's simply a natural reflex.

The "Can a Machine Tickle?" experiment sounds ridiculous but it may help answer an age-old stumper: Why can't we tickle ourselves? Many scientists currently believe that tickling is a reflex that requires anticipation and surprise. In order to tickle yourself, you'd need to be able to surprise yourself. Sound easy? Try jumping in front of a mirror and shouting, "Boo!" Not very shocking, is it?

Literal-Minded Professors

It's raining cats and dogs.

It's as light as a feather.

It's as easy as pie.

These are examples of figures of speech. Everyone knows that cats and dogs don't fall from the sky. Things that are said to be as "light as a feather" usually aren't. And what exactly about pie is easy? Figures of speech are meant to be taken with a grain of salt. No! We don't mean with an actual grain of salt! We mean that figures of speech aren't meant to be taken *literally*. Yet, some scientists have turned figures of speech into tongue-in-cheek research studies, making mountains out of molehills, you might say.

For example, you may have heard the expression, "That's like comparing apples to oranges!" This figure of speech is used when two unlike things are being compared, like day and night or, um, apples and oranges. After hearing this phrase for years, Scott Sandford, an astrophysicist at the NASA Ames Research Center in California, finally decided to scientifically compare apples and oranges. He dried out an apple and an orange, ground them down into powders, and used an instrument called a spectrometer to analyze the components of his samples. (We won't go into spectrometry, but you're probably familiar with a similar

More alike than you think.

phenomenon in which water droplets in the air separate the components of sunlight into a multicolored spectrum called a rainbow.)

Sandford's experiment proved that apples and oranges can be compared, after all. In fact, looking at the "infrared transmission spectra" of the two fruits, it's hard to tell them apart!

Taking another figure of speech literally, Mark Fonstad and William Pugatch of Texas State University and Brandon Vogt of Arizona State University used science to answer the nonsense question, "Is Kansas really as flat as a pancake?"

Which is flatter, a pancake or the state of Kansas? *Weird Science* has the answer.

The trio of scientists went to a local International House of Pancakes and bought a sample. Analyzing their pancake close up, they found that it wasn't very flat at all. Comparing the pancake results to data on Kansas from a United States Geological Survey, the team confirmed that Kansas was significantly flatter. So if you're ever in Kansas—or if you live in Kansas—you can now say with absolute confidence that the state is flatter than a pancake. Hooray for science!

Another figure of speech is also a famously unsolvable riddle: Which came first, the chicken or the egg? Determined to find an answer, Alice Shirrell Kaswell, a writer for the *Annals of Improbable Research*, mailed a chicken and an egg in separate packages. The chicken and the egg traveled from Cambridge, Massachusetts, to New York City by post. Kaswell took the same trip by train and waited for the results. A couple of days later, she announced that the chicken came before the egg. To be precise, it beat the egg by eleven hours and six minutes.

Hmm. More silly than scientific, but that's what we'd expect from the *Annals of Improbable Research*. A more rigorous theory recently emerged from England. Dr. Colin Freeman of Sheffield University used a supercomputer to show that eggshells are made with a protein found only in chickens. Without chickens, we wouldn't have eggs. Therefore, the chicken must have come first, right? Maybe. Scientists are still debating the issue, so don't count your chickens before they've hatched (unless you do it with a supercomputer and publish a nonsense scientific study about your findings).

Shooting for the Moon

For billions of years, the moon has been hanging around Earth like a little kid brother who won't go away. Yet, despite the fact that the moon and Earth go way back, mathematician Alexander Abian (1923–1999) suggested that the relationship be put to an end, once and for all.

Abian insisted that the moon wasn't worth the trouble it caused. He complained that its gravitational pull made Earth wobble and that the wobble led to extreme weather such as hurricanes, heat waves, and blizzards. His recommendation was that we get rid of it by blowing it up with nuclear missiles! Without a moon to mess up our forecasts, the weather would always be perfect. Abian even hinted that the nuking of the moon would be an impressive fireworks display.

Fortunately for us and the moon, no one took Abian's "Moonless Earth theory" seriously. Skeptical scientists predicted that if we blew up the moon, our planet would be ravaged by earthquakes and probably pelted by moon shrapnel, which would snuff out all life. Would the weather be nicer? Perhaps. But no one would be around to enjoy it.

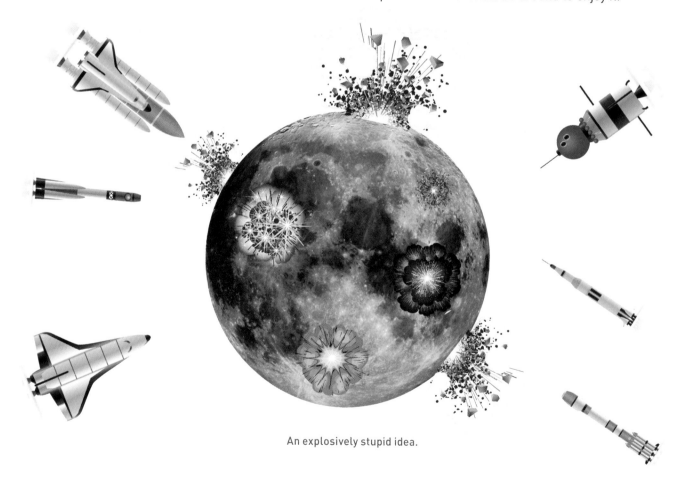

An explosively stupid idea.

Out of Their Orbits

According to most scientists, human activities such as driving around in gas-guzzling cars have caused Earth's surface temperature to rise. This increase in temperature is called global warming, and if it isn't stopped we might be confronted with catastrophes such as droughts, floods, violent storms, and possibly the extinction of many species of plants and animals. A group of engineers at the NASA Ames Research Center in California has come up with an ambitious solution: move Earth to a cooler spot!

It sounds impossible but the scientists believe that it can be done. They point out that spaceships sometimes get a boost from the gravitational pull of large objects. They propose to use this technique (called *gravity assist*) to nudge Earth away from the sun. Their plan sounds like something straight out of a sci-fi disaster movie. We send asteroids hurtling past Earth, and each asteroid would have a slight effect on our planet's orbit. Thousands of passing asteroids might get Earth out of the heat and undo the impact of global warming.

It sounds almost believable, but the more we think about it, the queasier we get. Human-made asteroid showers? Scientists fiddling with Earth's orbit? Maybe cutting down on gasoline would be a better solution to global warming.

Can asteroids rescue us from global warming?

Houston, we have a problem. . . a very big problem.

The Chimp and the Child

There are tales (some supposedly true) about children raised in the wild among wolves or apes or bears. Most of the stories are similar. The "wild child" is discovered and brought to civilization. Having never learned to speak, the child grunts or barks and continues to act wolflike or apelike or bearlike even after entering human society.

Winthrop Niles Kellogg (1898–1972), a psychologist living in Florida, was fascinated by cases of children raised by animals in the wild. Inspired by these stories, he posed a very odd question: If a boy raised as an ape will act like an ape, would an ape raised as a human act like a human?

In 1931, Kellogg began an experiment, hoping to find an answer. He decided to adopt a seven-month-old baby girl chimpanzee named Gua and bring her home to live with him, his wife, and his son, Donald, who was ten months old.

Donald the boy and Gua the chimp were treated as equals. They ate the same meals, played with the same toys, and were dressed in the same clothes. Every day, the scientist tested the babies to track their development. He tickled them to see how they'd react. (They giggled.)

Dr. Monkey Business.

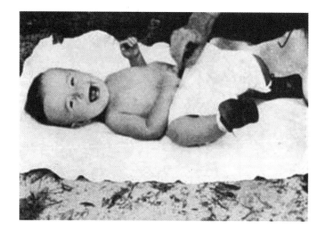

He spun them in chairs and filmed them getting dizzy. He subjected them to language tests, coordination tests, and memory tests. He even dangled treats on strings in a race-to-the-cookie test.

The results? Gua developed some very human habits. She ate from a spoon, drank from a glass, and learned to walk on two legs. On the downside, she was a bad influence on her older brother. At an age when most kids are learning to speak, Donald was grunting and cackling like a monkey. Taking other cues from his simian sister, he carried objects around in his mouth. He sometimes bit people and he began walking less and crawling more.

Fearing that Gua was making a monkey out of Donald, the Kelloggs stopped the experiment. Gua was sent back to the primate research center, where we assume she quickly unlearned all of her fancy human tricks. Kellogg's strange study proves that, if given the opportunity, kids will act like chimpanzees. But we already knew that, didn't we?

Uh-oh!

Note to future scientists: don't experiment on your kids!

FREAKY PHYSICS

What is physics? Imagine spending a day with a curious four-year-old who won't stop asking you questions. "Why is the sky blue? How do lightbulbs light up? What are stars? Why do magnets stick together? Where does the sun go at night? If I swing myself really fast, can I flip over the top of the swing set?"

These are all physics questions. And we're not going to answer them here, but we will say that, even if you swing very quickly, you'll never make it over the top of the set, unless, of course, you have little rockets strapped to your ankles. And if you're wondering how rockets work, that's physics, too!

Physics is the study of matter, energy, space, and time. It tries to explain the way the universe behaves. Physicists are scientists who study physics, and, as you can imagine, their work isn't so easy. ("Explain the universe!" How's that for a job description?)

We here at Weird Central aren't physicists, but we appreciate the weirdness of physics, so we've gathered together some physics-related strangeness for you. Read on and maybe some of these tidbits of freaky physics will come in handy the next time you're trapped with a curious four-year-old.

Weird Relativity

British physicist, mathematician, and all-around weird dude Sir Isaac Newton (see page 39) published his Laws of Motion in 1687. According to the first law, a body at rest will stay at rest unless acted upon by an outside force. And a body in motion will stay in motion unless acted upon by an outside force. In other words, on a flat road, your bike won't move until you start peddling, and, once you start peddling, it won't stop until you hit the brakes.

Okay. There's nothing particularly weird about that. But two hundred years after Newton, Albert Einstein came along to shake things up. A German scientist with a mad scientist hairdo, Einstein proposed some bewildering corrections to Newton's laws for objects traveling at extremely high speeds. According to Einstein's theory of relativity, the faster you travel, the heavier you would get. Weirder still, at high speeds not only would you get heavier but your watch would run more slowly. Time would slow down. And you would grow smaller. But you couldn't measure the difference with a ruler because the ruler would also be smaller.

At everyday speeds, these differences are too small to measure. However, if you had an identical twin who was traveling near the speed of light in a souped-up spaceship, then, theoretically, your sci-fi astronaut twin would become smaller and heavier and would age more slowly than you.

Albert Einstein reportedly once said, "You do not really understand something unless you can explain it to your grandmother." Well, we tried explaining the theory of relativity to our grandmothers and it didn't go very well. If you're a budding physicist, please read up on Einstein's theories and explain them to your grandmother. Then maybe your grandmother can explain them to us!

Twins separated at birth?

Why Is the Sky Blue?

Okay, so if you have an annoying four-year-old kid at your heels demanding to know why the sky is blue, here's the reason: Even though sunlight looks white, it's actually made up of all the colors of the rainbow. Each color has a different wavelength, with blue having the shortest. Light travels in a straight line unless it is reflected in a mirror, bent in a prism, or scattered by the gas molecules in the atmosphere. So, the light from the sun is scattered by Earth's atmosphere, and blue is scattered more than any of the other colors because of its short, choppy waves. Got it? Good luck with that four-year-old!

Friction Facts

Now, to be perfectly honest, you won't coast along on your bike forever after an initial push because of a little thing called *friction*. This is when two things rub against each other, slowing each other down. So, in this case, the ground eventually slows the bicycle wheels down. Applying the brakes creates *friction* between the wheel rims and the rubber brake pads, leading to a quicker stop. Just be careful not to press the front wheel brakes first!

Does Time Run Faster in Space?

Einstein made another odd prediction. He suggested that the gravitational force of a massive object like Earth would slow down time. In other words, he predicted that time would run faster in space. Was he right?

Before we answer that question, here's another. Are you familiar with GPS devices in cars? (If you aren't, imagine driving around with a funny computer voice telling you when to make turns and then saying, "Recalculating!" after you miss them.)

GPS stands for Global Positioning System. Drivers who use GPS devices are getting instructions from satellites, which are orbiting Earth. If Einstein was correct, then time should run a little bit faster in GPS satellites.

And that's exactly what happens. It's been determined that, each day, GPS satellites gain a tiny fraction of a second. It might sound inconsequential, but this miniscule difference would cause GPS systems to be off by about six miles per day! How do GPS satellites handle this problem? Simple! The satellites come equipped with special slow-running clocks. Time runs faster in space. So, once the satellites are in orbit, these slow clocks slow down until they're running exactly the same as clocks on Earth.

Astronaut Marsha Ivins proves that in free fall, every day is a bad hair day.

Zero-Gravity Tourism

Science-fiction fans Noah Fulmor and Erin Finnegan of Brooklyn, New York, wanted to have an unusual wedding. Getting married on Mars was out of the question, so they picked the next best thing: a wedding aboard a Boeing 727 airplane, specially converted with padded walls and padded floors so that passengers could experience weightlessness without getting hurt. The plane was supplied by Zero Gravity Corporation (or ZERO-G), a company that specializes in zero-gravity tourism.

Like all weddings, a lot of planning was involved. But Fulmor and Finnegan had some extra details to work out. The bride had wires in her hair to keep it from drifting in front of her face, and the groom bought an extra-stiff, no-float tuxedo.

The wedding took place on June 20, 2009, and everything went according to plan, except for the ZERO-G wedding kiss. Unfortunately, the floating groom accidentally gave the floating bride a bump on the nose. But all marriages have their rough spots, don't they?

So, how does the plane allow passengers to experience weightlessness? It doesn't fly into space. It only goes about 36,000 feet above the ground. A space shuttle orbiting earth is about thirty times farther away. (And even in the space shuttle, astronauts aren't truly weightless. At a distance of two hundred miles from Earth, gravity is only weakened by a little bit, so a 160-pound astronaut would still weigh about 140 pounds.)

Answer: The passengers in the ZERO-G plane feel weightless because the plane arcs up and down like a roller coaster. When the plane is diving, the passengers and the plane are in free fall, so they experience weightlessness. And the astronauts in the space shuttle are also experiencing weightlessness because the shuttle orbiting Earth is free-falling. It's actually falling around Earth!

Have you ever gone over a hill in a car and bounced up in your seat with a queasy feeling in your stomach? If you have, you experienced a moment of weightlessness, just like the couple on the ZERO-G plane. But remember that queasy feeling before you schedule a ZERO-G party. Astronauts in training missions have a nickname for the planes that take them on these weightless roller-coaster rides. They call them Vomit Comets.

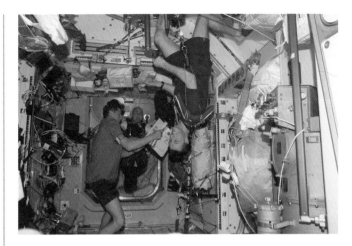

Astronauts on the International Space Station.

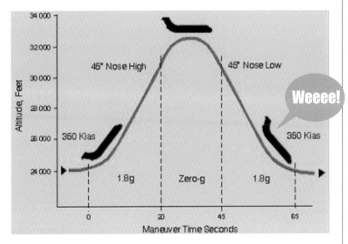

Zero-gravity flight trajectory.

You can experience free-fall weightlessness on Vomit Comets right here on Earth.

The Human Centrifuge

If you're sitting on a chair reading this book, then you're experiencing a g-force of 1. In other words, the force of the chair holding you up exactly matches the force of Earth's gravity pushing you down. If we take away the chair, then you'd be free-falling with a g-force of zero. That is, until you hit the floor. Ouch!

If you're curious what it's like to experience a g-force greater than 1, imagine that you're reading this book while blasting off in a rocket ship. As the rocket accelerates, you would feel a strong force, pushing you down into your seat. Pressed tightly against the cushions, you might even find it hard to move!

What's the greatest g-force a human can withstand? That's a question scientists were trying to answer back in the 1950s, in the early days of space travel. To help with this research, the U.S. Navy built a fantastic machine inside a base near Philadelphia. Like an out-of-control, high-speed amusement-park ride, the Human Centrifuge trained and tested future astronauts by spinning them around, faster and faster, so that they could experience extremely high g-forces.

A spin in the Human Centrifuge may sound like fun, but it was dangerous and hard on the human body. As you would expect, astronauts grew to dread the Human Centrifuge even more than the Vomit Comet. But Dr. R. Flanagan Gray, a physician working on the project, refused to let crushing speeds slow down his research.

He was convinced that people could withstand higher g-forces if they were surrounded by water. Dr. Gray ran some experiments riding the centrifuge at high speeds while sloshing around inside a water tank. The tank was nicknamed the "Blue Shoe," but it didn't really look like a shoe. It was more like a big metal bathtub. His work eventually led to a wonderfully weird invention: a strange suit called the "Iron Maiden." Unlike diving suits, which are designed to keep water out, the Iron Maiden held water in!

The 20-G Centrifuge at NASA's Ames Research Center in Moffett Field, California.

In 1958, the doctor, holding his breath inside his water-filled suit, rode the Human Centrifuge up to 31.25 g's. His eyesight and balance weren't the same afterward, but he survived. A world record was established, and, to this day, it hasn't been broken.

Nowadays, the former naval base is open to the public. If you're in Warminster, Pennsylvania, make sure to stop for a tour at the Johnsville Centrifuge and Science Museum. You won't be able to ride in the Human Centrifuge, but you can sit inside it. And afterward, you might be able to snag a T-shirt that says, "I Went to 1 g in the Centrifuge." Of course, we know that going to 1 g is highly unimpressive, but at least you can do it without a special suit filled with water.

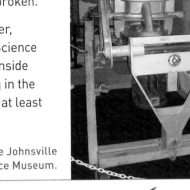

The Iron Maiden on display at the Johnsville Centrifuge and Science Museum.

The Crack or the Jet?

Here's a silly question you probably won't get in physics class (unless your teacher is a fellow weirdo): Imagine a race between two very speedy opponents—Challenger #1, a crack moving through a huge sheet of glass, and Challenger #2, the world's fastest jet plane, shrieking through the sky—which is faster, the crack or the jet?

Answer: A crack travels through glass at more than 3,000 miles per hour. The official speed record for a manned jet, set by the Lockheed SR-71 on July 28, 1976, was 2,193.2 miles per hour.

But wait! If you were rooting for the crack, don't start cheering just yet. (And incidentally, why were you rooting for a crack?)

Wanna race?

Some people believe that a faster manned jet was designed in the 1980s or 1990s. It was supposedly called the SR-91 Aurora. Skeptics insist that the Aurora doesn't exist. Believers argue that the plane was completed, but the Aurora project was canceled so that research could move ahead on unmanned aircrafts and satellites. However, in the 1990s, a series of strange sonic booms was detected in California. Some conspiracy theorists are convinced that these booms were created by the secret testing of a supersonic aircraft like the mysterious Aurora. If this was true, then seismologists predict that the aircraft would have been traveling between 3,000 and 4,000 miles per hour.

So it's a close contest between a crack and a possibly nonexistent aircraft. It's Weird Science, so what else would you expect?

You crack me up.

The Tacoma Narrows Bridge Disaster

The original Tacoma Narrows Bridge opened on July 1, 1940. Spanning the Tacoma Narrows in Washington State, it was 5,939 feet long. The bridge was quickly given the nickname "Galloping Gertie" because it was known to twist, turn, and ripple in the wind. Motorists who had driven across the bridge often compared the trip to a roller-coaster ride. Some even hit waves big enough to make them lose sight of the cars in front of them. If you're thinking that it's a bad sign for a bridge to get a nickname like Galloping Gertie, you're absolutely right.

On November 7, 1940, four months after the bridge opened, it collapsed. No one died, but a small dog and a few abandoned cars went tumbling into the waters below. The suspension bridge had been designed to handle winds up to 120 miles per hour, but the wind on that day was only 42 miles per hour. What caused the Tacoma Narrows Bridge to collapse?

Most scientists today point to a phenomenon called *aeroelastic flutter*. This means that there was some kind of weird feedback loop between the constant wind and the vibrating bridge, until the vibrations became too much for the bridge to handle.

Fortunately, the story has a happy ending. The bridge was rebuilt, and a second, twin bridge added next to it later. The first new, safe, and improved Tacoma Narrows Bridge was opened on October 14, 1950, and the sister bridge opened on July 15, 2007. To our knowledge, neither has been called Galloping Gertie.

Static Electricity or . . . ZAP!

Have you ever combed your hair and seen little sparks? No? Well, try combing your hair in the dark in front of a mirror. (If anyone asks, just tell them you're doing a physics experiment!) Or have you ever scuffed your feet on the carpet and then gotten a shock when you touched a doorknob? These shocks and sparks are electrostatic discharges. Everything, including your feet and the carpet, is made up of atoms, and atoms are made of positively charged protons; negatively charged electrons; and neutrons, which have no charge.

Going Down

These days, the Tacoma Narrows Bridge, known as "Sturdy Gertie," and its sister look a lot safer.

Static electricity in action.

Electrons and protons follow two laws, which are easy to remember. Like charges repel each other, and opposite charges attract. In other words, two electrons will pull away from each other, whereas an electron and a proton will pull toward each other.

Most of the time, atoms are balanced. They have the same number of protons and electrons, so the positive and negative charges cancel each other out. But if an atom gains extra electrons it becomes negatively charged, and you have static electricity.

That's what happened to you when you walked across the carpet. You picked up electrons and became imbalanced (electrostatically speaking, of course!). Metal doorknobs are conductors. So when you touched the doorknob, the extra electrons jumped from your finger to the knob, and . . . zap!

Try It Yourself: A Sticky Experiment

If you want to learn about static electricity without shocking anyone, here's a simple experiment. All you need is a roll of transparent tape (the kind you use when wrapping presents). Peel off two pieces about six inches long. Stick them on a smooth surface like a table or a desk and then rip them off. (But before you do, check with an adult to make sure that the surface won't get ruined by the tape. You don't want to leave any unwanted tape marks!) You'll now have two negatively charged pieces of tape. Hold them near each other, side by side, and let them dangle. They won't hang straight down. Instead, they'll bend away from each other. This is because like charges repel.

For another experiment, stick two pieces of tape together and then pull them apart quickly. Now, one will be more positively charged than the other. Opposite charges attract, so when you hold up the two pieces, side by side, again, what do you think will happen? Instead of repelling, they will pull toward each other.

Lightning is another example of static electricity. In this case, the imbalance of charges is created by air rubbing against rain clouds.

Tape Rays

And here's another weird physics fact about tape: scientists at UCLA recently experimented with transparent tape and found that electromagnetic radiation was emitted when tape was pulled from its dispenser. The radiation has a name that you're probably familiar with: X-rays. Don't worry, you don't need a lead vest every time you reach for the tape. It only works in a vacuum, which means if air is present, you won't get X-rays. Still, the scientists at UCLA were able to use tape radiation to X-ray someone's finger!

The Van de Graaff Generator

In 1929, American physicist Robert J. Van de Graaff created an amazing device known as the Van de Graaff generator. It looks like a metal sphere resting on a tall, thin column. When it's turned on, the metal sphere becomes charged and the generator can demonstrate static electricity in action.

Van de Graaff generators can be used to create spectacular lightning shows. They can also make your hair stand on end! If you touch the sphere of a Van de Graaff generator, your hair will become charged. Each charged strand of hair will repel the strand beside it, so your hair will rise, making you look like a big, dandelion puffball. Still, looking silly is a small price to pay when you're demonstrating the wonders of science!

Van de Graaff generators can be found in cheesy old science-fiction movies (usually in mad-scientist labs). They are also on display in science museums across the country. The world's largest is in the Museum of Science in Boston, Massachusetts, and it can produce up to two million volts of electricity!

A Van de Graaff generator.

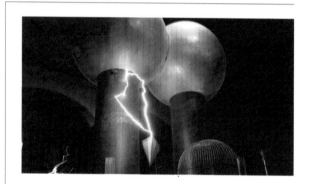

The largest Van de Graaff generator in the world—located at the Museum of Science in Boston, Massachusetts.

The Museum of Science in Boston, Massachusetts.

The Universe Is (Mostly) Empty

Did you know that the universe, and everything in it, is mostly just empty space? It sounds impossible, but it's true.

A brick wall may look solid to you. And if you bump into one, it would certainly feel solid. But bricks, like everything else, are made of atoms, and atoms are made of protons, electrons, and neutrons. However, atoms are mostly just empty space. In fact, they're 99.99999999 percent nothing!

To make it easier to understand, we'll explain what we mean in baseball terms. If an atom were the size of a baseball field, the nucleus, which contains the protons and the neutrons, would be about as big as a bug crawling on home plate. And the electrons would be like flecks of dust in the air.

So why does the brick wall seem so solid? Protons and electrons attracting each other. Electrons and electrons repelling each other. These electrostatic forces hold everything together and, sadly, make it impossible for you to walk through brick walls.

That's right, this brick wall is mostly empty space. You still don't want to bang your head on it, though.

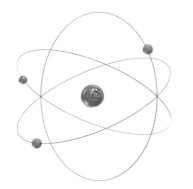

A model of an atom: a whole bunch of nearly nothing.

The Mars Club

Since the 1960s, thirty-eight probes have been launched from Earth with Mars as their destination. Only nineteen have been successful. The failure rate is so high that it has been given a nickname: the Mars Curse. And in 1997, *Time* magazine writer Donald Neff concocted a ridiculous story to explain what was happening to all of those probes. According to Neff, a space monster called the Galactic Ghoul was eating them. How do we improve our luck with Mars exploration and conquer the Galactic Ghoul?

Members of a group called the Mars Club have a simple answer. They believe we've been relying too much on unmanned space missions. They insist that humans could resolve problems that might stump robots and computers. Most space researchers disagree, arguing that manned flights would be dangerous and expensive. In other words, humans may be clever, but robots are easier to care for.

The Mars Club—also known as the Association of Mars Explorers—has members around the world and meets regularly to discuss Mars research.

This is what the Mars Climate Orbiter should have looked like as it orbited Mars in 1999. However, one of the engineers working on the program failed to convert metric units into standard measurement and the orbiter was destroyed in Mars's atmosphere.

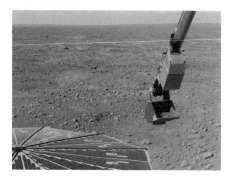

Members also travel to harsh places like Antarctica and the Arctic, seeking out weird Mars-like environments on Earth.

Many of the Mars Clubbers share a common dream. They hope to someday reach Mars themselves and perhaps spend their final days there.

If you're obsessed with all things Martian and hope to visit your favorite planet someday, maybe the Mars Club is the club for you. Check out www.marsexplorers.org for details. But remember, the Galactic Ghoul is out there and it's hungry!

The successful missions to Mars have provided amazing clues to this mysterious planet, as well as some amazing photos. The image below is of Victoria Crater on Mars. It was taken by the Mars Exploration Rover Opportunity in 2006. The image above right was taken by Phoenix, a robotic spacecraft that landed on Mars in 2008.

Looking Back in Time

When you look up at a star, you're not actually seeing the star. You're looking at light that left the star some time ago. For example, it takes a little over eight minutes for light from the sun to arrive at Earth. Light from a faraway star may have traveled for years. In fact, scientists measure a star's distance by the number of years it takes for the star's light to reach us.

After the sun, the next closest star is Proxima Centauri, which is 4.3 light years away. Other stars are millions of light years away, so when you look through a telescope, you're actually looking millions of years backward in time! But just how far back can we look?

To answer that question, here's a recent development: there's a spaceship called the Wilkinson Microwave Anisotropy Probe (or WMAP), also known as the Microwave Anisotropy Probe (MAP), also known as Explorer 80. (Come on, guys! One name per spaceship, please!) In 2003, WMAP detected cosmic microwave background radiation from close to when the universe was born, more than 13 billion years ago. NASA scientists called the radiation a "baby picture" of the universe. Was the universe a cute baby? We'll leave that to you to decide.

Now, that's some old light you're looking at!

Those are some cute baby pictures you've got there!

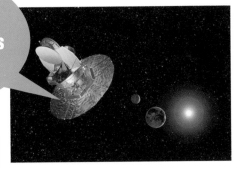

A drawing of WMAP on its journey one million miles beyond Earth.

The Demotion of Pluto and Other Sad Stories

How many planets are in our solar system? Answer: Eight—Mercury, Venus, Earth, Mars, Jupiter, Saturn, Uranus, and Neptune.

If you're wondering what happened to Pluto, it was demoted. In August 2006, the General Assembly of the International Astronomical Union decided that Pluto was no longer a planet. They weren't punishing Pluto for misbehaving or anything like that. The problem was that Pluto just wasn't big enough. Instead of being a planet, Pluto is now considered a dwarf planet. There are more than forty other possible dwarf planets in our solar system, and they have names like Ceres, Haumea, Eris, and Makemake. (For Pluto's sake, we hope that silly Makemake never gets promoted to planet status. That would be too embarrassing!)

This news is yet another bad break for a very unlucky astronomer named Percival Lawrence Lowell (1855–1916). Lowell was convinced that there were canals on Mars and even wrote a book called *Mars and Its Canals*. He was wrong. Toward the end of his life, Lowell tirelessly searched for a new planet, which he called Planet X. He never found Planet X, but fourteen years after his death, in 1930, Clyde Tombaugh, working at

Percival Lawrence Lowell, hard at work.

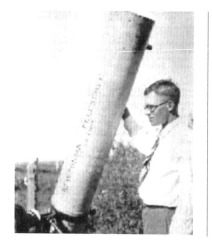

Clyde *Tombaugh*'s planet was demoted in 2006.

the Lowell Observatory in Arizona, discovered a new planet. Tombaugh named it Pluto—partly because Pluto was the name of the Roman god of the underworld and also because Pluto began with *pl*, the initials of Percival Lowell.

Let's tip our caps to the unlucky Pluto and Percival Lowell. There are only eight planets again, so the search for Planet X continues!

Can I catch a break here?

The Lowell Observatory

If you'd like to see the Pluto Discovery Telescope that Clyde Tombaugh used, it's exhibited in the Lowell Observatory in Flagstaff, Arizona. The observatory also showcases several other telescopes and is currently building the Discovery Channel Telescope, which will be the fifth largest in the country. According to the plans, it will be seventy-eight feet tall and sixty-two feet wide, and the telescope's mirror will weigh 6,700 pounds!

Black Holes, Wormholes, and the Marvelous Multiverse

We here at Weird Central are science-fiction fans, and we have closets full of *Star Wars* memorabilia to prove it. If you're also into sci-fi, then you've probably heard of black holes and wormholes. What you may not know is that these weird concepts come from a branch of science called *astrophysics*, which is the physics behind planets and galaxies, stars and solar systems.

What is a black hole? Imagine a star, ten times bigger than the sun, going supernova. (That's a scientific term that means . . . *kaboom*!) Then imagine, after the explosion, the star collapsing inward from its own gravitational forces. The star collapses until it's infinitely tiny and so dense that nothing that gets close to it, not even light, can escape its gravitational pull.

And here's where our brains start going numb. Some astrophysicists have suggested that the gravitational forces of black holes create tiny tunnels out in space. These strange shortcuts are called *wormholes*. According to scientists, wormholes are probably too small for people to squeeze through. Theoretical astrophysicist Stephen Hawking estimates that they're only about a billion-trillion-trillionth of a centimeter in size. Still, he supposes that someday, it might be possible for space travelers to use wormholes to travel from one point of the universe to another.

Weirder still, a wormhole might lead to another time—into the future or into the distant past, to the time of the dinosaurs. Or perhaps a wormhole could lead to another universe entirely! This brings us to possibly the most bizarre concept of all: multiple universes!

According to some very imaginative scientists, our universe might be one of an infinite number of universes, all crowded together like soap bubbles in a bubble bath. This weird universe of universes is called the *multiverse*, and theoretically it contains an infinite number of versions of all of us. And by now, I'm sure that we're all completely confused.

An illustration of what a black hole might look like.

Supernova! This dead star in the constellation Taurus was observed on Earth in the year 1054.

Stephen Hawking

MEDICAL MARVELS & MISHAPS

One of the earliest forms of surgery extends back to prehistoric times. It's called *trepanation* and here's how it worked: If Caveman #1 had a headache, Caveman #2 would relieve the pressure by punching a hole in the skull of Caveman #1. If Caveman #1 survived the "operation," he could keep the removed skull fragment as a souvenir.

Fast-forward thousands of years to the ancient Greeks. They believed that the human body was kept in balance by four humors: blood, phlegm, black bile, and yellow bile. (Yuck.) If Ancient Greek #1 felt sick, Ancient Greek #2 might have tried to even out the patient's humors by removing a few quarts of blood. How did they extract blood in ancient Greece? They often used handy little bloodsucking worms called leeches.

The field of medicine has come a long way since the days of skull drilling and bloodletting, but the journey has been very strange and full of miracles, mistakes, and more gross-out stories than you can possibly imagine.

Case in point: leeches are making a comeback! It seems that leech saliva stops blood from clotting. So, if you lose an ear and need to have it sewn back on, don't be surprised if your doctor reaches for a jar full of writhing, bloodsucking, creepy-crawly worms.

Hold on to your ears and watch out for leeches! We present to you a small sampling of marvels and mishaps from medical history.

A trepanated skull from around 2,000 years ago. Scientists determined that the person with this hole in his or her head survived the operation.

This portrait shows Dr. John Clarke demonstrating his trepanning technique. He was one of the first doctors to perform a trepanation operation in North America.

Um . . . never mind, Doctor. I'm feeling much better. Really!

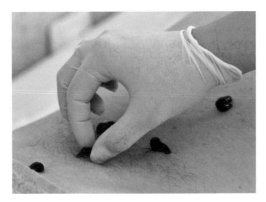

Leeches making a comeback!

Our Weird Brains

We'll start off with a few brain-related medical oddities, but first we'd like you to embarrass yourself by reading the next sentence aloud.

"The human brain is very weird!"

Done? Okay. Here's what just happened. The information in the sentence was sent to the visual cortex in your brain. It was decoded in your Wernicke's area and zipped along to your Broca's area, which created instructions for your motor cortex, which then moved your lips and everything else that moved when you spoke.

The study of the brain is called *neuroscience*, and, as you might expect, neuroscience is fascinating and unbelievably complicated. Your brain has about a hundred billion nerve cells (called *neurons*) and each cell is connected to thousands of other cells, and these connections help your nerve cells deliver electrical and chemical signals with messages such as, "Let's eat!" or "Let's read a book about weird science!"

Maggot Madness

Live maggots were used by the Mayans, the Aboriginal tribes in Australia, and other ancient civilizations to treat wounds and keep infection at bay. Today, maggots are once again being used to remove dead tissue and aid in healing wounds. They're also used to treat ulcers, gangrene, skin cancer, and burns. Surgeons may use them after an operation to decrease the risk of infection. In 2004, the Food and Drug Administration (FDA) classified leeches and maggots as the first live medical devices.

When your neurons are firing, information speeds through your brain, traveling as fast as 268 miles per hour. Different regions in your brain have different functions. Thinking happens in the frontal cortex. Your emotions come from an area called the limbic region, and your brain stem is responsible for the stuff you do without thinking. It keeps your heart pumping and your stomach digesting, and it makes sure that you never forget to breathe.

So as you read these words, you may not think you're doing much, but there's a lot going on behind the scenes. What a wonderful, weird, and very busy brain you have!

The Amazing Case of Phineas Gage

A horrible accident took place in Cavendish, Vermont, on September 13, 1848. A construction team was blasting through rocks, making way for a railroad. They drilled a hole in the stone, same as they always did. Then the construction foreman, a handsome twenty-five-year-old New Hampshire man named Phineas Gage, stepped up to finish the job. Gage poured in blasting powder and a fuse, tossed in some sand, and packed it all down with a long, iron tamping rod.

Suddenly . . . BOOM!

An explosion sent the rod flying high into the air, and the unfortunate construction foreman collapsed to the ground. His hands and clothes were burned and his head was bleeding. The tamping rod landed with a clank nearly eighty feet away. It was bloody and speckled with brain matter.

The situation looked grim for Gage. The rod, which was three feet, seven inches long and an inch and a quarter wide, had passed through his head, entering in just below his left eye and exiting out from the top of his skull.

Yet, despite the fact that he had a hole clear through his head, Gage was still alive. In fact, just minutes after the incident, he was talking. He was even able to walk! Carefully, his men led him to a cart and, sitting up in it, shaky but wide awake, Gage rode to the lodge in town where he was staying and waited for a doctor to arrive.

The local doctor was a physician named Dr. John Harlow. During his examination, he cleared away pieces of bone. He poked his fingers through the holes and touched his fingertips together inside Gage's head. The doctor's worst suspicions were confirmed!

Gage drifted in and out of consciousness for the next month, but, little by little, against all expectations, his health improved. As you'd imagine, there were side effects. One, of course, was a big dent in his head. Besides that, his eyesight wasn't the same and his balance was off. Other side effects were weirder. Actually they were more than weird, and they've made Phineas Gage a legend in the world of medicine.

Phineas Gage's personality was transformed. Before his injury, he had been a model worker and a good leader, responsible, reliable, and very smart. Afterward, he was different. As his friends put it, he was "no longer Gage." He couldn't follow through on his promises, and he was no longer polite and agreeable. Instead, he was unpredictable, foulmouthed, restless, and stubborn. A liar. An argument starter. A tantrum thrower. (Although, to be fair, if you had a hole in your head, wouldn't you be a bit moody?)

Dr. Harlow guessed that the changes in Gage's personality were a result of brain damage. At the time, this idea was quite shocking. Not much was known about the human brain in the mid-1800s, and many people believed in a silly theory called *phrenology*. According to phrenology, your personality is determined by the shape of your head, not by the brain inside it.

Gage's tamping rod and skull—housed in the Warren Anatomical Museum at Harvard University School of Medicine.

Today, we know that Dr. Harlow was right. The part of Gage's brain that was damaged is called the *ventromedial nucleus*. And modern researchers have confirmed that damage to this area can cause a shift in a patient's personality, similar to the transformation in the strange case of Phineas Gage.

What happened to Phineas Gage? We know that, because of his wild behavior, the railroad refused to give him back his old job, and so, after ten weeks of rest and recuperation, he returned to his parents' house in Lebanon, New Hampshire. From there, the story gets hazy and it's hard to separate the truth from the legend. Some say that Phineas Gage joined the famous Barnum & Bailey Circus and performed in Barnum's New York City Odditorium as a featured attraction: The Only Living Man with a Hole in His Head.

Strangely, Gage grew very fond of the tamping rod that had caused so much trouble. "My iron bar," he called it. It became almost like a companion to him in his later years. Growing weaker and suffering from epileptic seizures, Gage spent his final days in San Francisco, living with his mother. He died on May 21, 1860, almost twelve years after the accident.

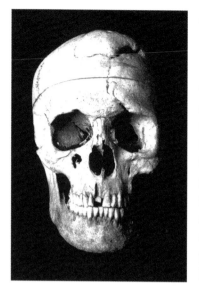

The Warren Anatomical Museum

If you're fascinated by the strange tale of Phineas Gage, you may want to take a trip to the Warren Anatomical Museum, located on the fifth floor of the Countway Library of Medicine in Boston, Massachusetts. Phineas Gage's skull is on display, along with the famous tamping rod and a plaster cast of the man's head (hole included). And while you're at it, make sure to check out the collection of skeletons, kidney stones, and scary out-of-date medical tools (and breathe a sigh of relief that you weren't around when they were in use). Not for the squeamish, but not to be missed!

Synesthesia and the Brain

Close your eyes and imagine the number 4. In your mind, did the number have a color? Was it red like a cherry or green like a pickle? When you picture the word Saturday is it blue, like the sky? Does the sound of a tuba make you feel tingling in your cheek? Does the sight of a city skyline make you taste watermelon?

If so, you may have a condition called *synesthesia*. People with synesthesia are called synesthetes and they experience the world in an interesting way. Their senses are somehow joined together. They might smell shapes or see music or feel colors. Not all synesthetes are in synch. One might have a mental image of the letter A as being red. To another, the letter might be purple or gold.

If you have *synesthesia*, we have a few questions for you. How did you get to be so lucky? Which tastes better, the letter Q or the letter Z? What's going on inside that amazing brain of yours?

David Eagleman and a team of neuroscientists at the Baylor College Eagleman Laboratory in Texas were also curious about that last question. Looking for answers, they rounded up a group of synesthetes and began studying them. Dr. Eagleman asked the synesthetes to watch black-and-white episodes of *Sesame Street*. As the subjects gazed at the TV screen, the scientist recorded their brain activity.

Using magnetic resonance imaging (MRI), Eagleman and his team were able to see the brain of a synesthete in action. The colorless letters and

SYNESTHESIA
0123456789

numbers triggered two parts of the brain at once: the area that understands shapes and the area that recognizes colors. These two regions are separate but are positioned right beside each other.

The conclusion? Well, uh, we're not neuroscientists, so we can't say for sure, but Dr. Eagleman and his team showed that the synesthetes were not just imagining colors on a black-and-white TV. They were actually seeing colors. Or, at least, their brains were seeing colors. It seems that a synesthete has a wonderfully oversensitive brain. When one part of the brain starts firing, this causes a neighboring part to start firing. The result is a mental fireworks display of mixed sensations.

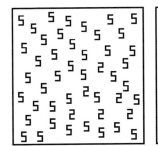

What most people see.

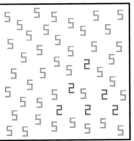

What you might see if you have synesthesia.

And if hearing shapes and smelling music aren't strange enough for you, how about the guy whose girlfriend's name tasted like broccoli? (Unfortunately, he wasn't a big fan of the vegetable.) Or how about the color-blind synesthete who could only see colors if he stared at numbers?

Head Games

In 1896, H. G. Wells wrote The *Island of Dr. Moreau*, a creepy tale about a mad doctor performing experiments on an uncharted island. Mixing and matching animals and people, the mad doctor created monstrosities like the Hyena-Swine and the Leopard Man.

The history of medicine is full of similarly horrifying experiments. Except the doctors involved weren't fictional like Dr. Moreau, and the experiments they conducted were real.

In the early 1900s, Charles Claude Guthrie became famous for his breakthroughs in vascular surgery, a surgical specialty involving veins and arteries. Unfortunately, his fame as a surgeon is now tarnished by a shocking experiment that he performed in 1908. He created the first-ever two-headed dog by surgically attaching the head of one dog onto the neck of another. The transplanted head barely moved.

More successful two-headed dog experiments were conducted in the 1950s by a Russian scientist named Vladimir Demikhov. He attached a puppy's head, along with its shoulders and lungs, onto a fully-grown dog.

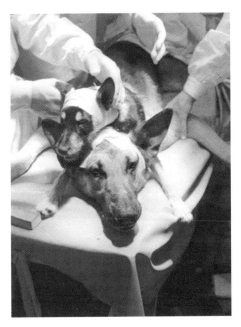

Dr. Demikhov's two-headed dog.

The transplanted puppy head lapped at milk (and even snapped at researchers). But Demikhov's two-headed beasts never survived long after surgery. The longest lasted a month.

Seeing Russians moving heads, Americans decided to rally and venture into a new, and very questionable, subject of study: head transplantation. For years, Dr. Robert White conducted preliminary experiments at a brain research lab at Case Western Reserve University in Cleveland, Ohio. On March 14, 1970, the scientist conducted a monkey-head transplant, successfully attaching the head of one monkey onto the body of another. Instead of fame, the bizarre experiment hurt the doctor's reputation and so his dreams of a human-head transplant never came to pass.

Is there a future for head transplantation? Probably not. Most likely, it's an area of medical research that has come and gone, and which now seems as barbaric and loony as the insane hybrid beast experiments of Dr. Moreau. Still, there is a remote chance that head transplantation will make a dramatic and very weird comeback.

Let's say that scientists work out the kinks involved with human-head transplantation surgery. Using cloning, they might also find a way to create unconscious but healthy, headless human bodies that could be harvested for spare parts. (Scientists have engineered headless mice and headless tadpoles, so this might not be as far out as you think). Imagine a future when someone becomes paralyzed after an accident or develops an incurable disease that affects his or her body. Or maybe the body is just old and feeble, but the brain is still as sharp as a tack. The person might go to the hospital, receive a head transplant, and leave with an entirely new body—possibly a cloned, headless version of him- or herself!

Headless humans? Old-for-new body exchange? Is this a future you'd actually want? Well, that's another question.

The Body Farm

If you're a fan of TV programs like *CSI* or *NCIS* (or any show with *C* for Criminal and *I* for Investigation in its name), then you've probably seen scenes like this: a body washes ashore and a special team of scientifically minded detectives comes to investigate; after examining the body, the team is able to determine roughly when the person died and if the death was an accident or due to foul play.

These kinds of scenes happen in real life, too. In fact, police detectives and medical examiners can learn an awful lot from a corpse just by the way it's decaying. Believe it or not, there is a branch of science devoted to the study of how human remains decompose. It's called *forensic anthropology*.

The Body Farm, where people are dying to get in.

In 1981, Dr. William Blass founded the Forensic Anthropology Center in Knoxville, Tennessee. The place is now legendary, partly because of its huge contribution to the field of forensic anthropology and partly because it's so shockingly weird.

The facility is a 2.5-acre outdoor lot surrounded by a tall barbed-wire fence to keep out unwanted visitors. Behind the barrier, scattered about the woods, clearing, and hillsides are corpses—dozens and dozens of corpses—in various stages of decomposition. Some are festering out in the open. Others are stuffed into car trunks, crammed into suitcases, lying in puddles, or buried in shallow graves. All in all, there are about 160 corpses rotting at the outdoor research lab at any given time.

The nightmarish sight and the overpowering stench would scare off most people, but scientists at the facility and forensic anthropology students aren't easily discouraged. Strolling from cadaver to cadaver, they're always busy collecting data, studying how quickly human bodies decompose in different situations. No detail is too gross. They pay special attention to the effects of weather and insect activity. It's all in a day's work at the Forensic Anthropology Center, better known by its catchier nickname—the Body Farm.

Waiting for the Body Farm

How does the Body Farm get its bodies? It receives donations. Not money, but corpses. Surprisingly, many people have requested the Body Farm as their final resting place. The farm receives more than a hundred new donations per year. There's even a waiting list to get in!

The facility has been so successful that, because of it, other medical schools around the country have opened "body farms." One at Texas State University was plagued by vultures scavenging its research subjects. The solution? Scientists decided to start gathering data on vulture activity. What else would you expect from forensic anthropologists?

Extra Innings for Teddy Ballgame?

"The Kid." "Teddy Ballgame." "Splendid Splinter."

These were all nicknames for baseball hall-of-famer Ted Williams. Williams ended the 1941 baseball season with a .406 batting average. Many Major Leaguers have played the game since then, but none have matched or beaten Williams's record. Yet, Williams is an important figure not only in the world of baseball but also in the world of the weird. Why? Because "The Kid" is now "The Frozen Kid." Ted Williams's remains are cryogenically preserved and stored at the Alcor Life Extension Foundation in Scottsdale, Arizona.

Cryonics is the practice of freezing dead people with the hopes that someday scientists of the future will figure out how to thaw them out and bring them back to life. Now, let's think about this for a second. . . .In order for cryonics to work, not only will the scientists of tomorrow have to figure out how to unfreeze human corpses without damaging the brains or internal organs, which is already is a lot to ask, but they will also have to discover how to bring the dead back to life!

Cryonics was first posed as a possible road to immortality in the 1960s. Since then it's gained a lot of supporters. Some cryonics supporters have died and had their bodies frozen. Others have frozen just their brains. The brain-only option in cryonics is called *neuropreservation*. In order for this scheme to work, doctors will someday have to figure out how to

(1) de-ice the brain,

(2) implant it into a new body, and

(3) bring the dead brain-implant patient back to life.

Whew! For the sake of the frozen brains out there, we hope that the doctors of the future are very, very smart!

How did a baseball legend like Ted Williams get mixed up with cryonics? The answer involves a soiled napkin, an unusual pact, and a little family drama.

Ted Williams died of a heart attack on July 5, 2002. In his will, he had asked to be cremated. Instead, his son, John-Henry, and his daughter, Claudia, had him frozen. To back up their decision, they presented a napkin with grease stains and scribbles on it. Signed by Ted Williams, John-Henry, and Claudia, the napkin was a "family pact" stating that the father, son, and daughter wanted to be cryogenically preserved. According to the brother and sister, this decision offered the family a faint hope of someday being together again.

Bobby Jo Ferrell, Ted's daughter from a previous marriage, insisted that her father had never agreed to be frozen. She was convinced that the napkin was a fake created by her half siblings. Despite her objections, the remains of Ted Williams were sent to the Alcor Life Extension Foundation. The baseball legend's head was removed and placed in a container the size of a large cooking pot. His body was stored in a big cylinder, and both the head-can and the body-tube were filled with liquid nitrogen, a fluid that instantaneously freezes anything that it touches. Less than two years later, the pop(sicle) was joined by his son. John-Henry Williams died of leukemia in March 2004 and is currently on ice at Alcor with his father.

Will scientists ever discover how to unfreeze the frozen, bring back the dead, and reunite the Williams family? Today, it seems impossible, but we'll never know for sure. There may be surprises to come in the story of Ted, John-Henry, and Claudia Williams. As another baseball hall-of-famer Yogi Berra liked to say, "It ain't over till it's over!"

THE WEIRD SCIENCE HALL OF SHAME

Chapter 8

On July 20, 1969, astronaut Neil Armstrong set his foot on the moon and spoke these famous words: "That's one small step for man, one giant leap for mankind." The history of science is full of giant leaps forward, flashes of inspiration, and moments of great discovery. Unfortunately, you won't find any of that stuff in this chapter. Instead, you'll find big steps backward, embarrassments, abominations, conspiracies, and hoaxes. Instead of geniuses, you will find con artists and nincompoops devoted to the pursuit of utter nonsense.

Set aside logic. Forget reason. In this chapter, everything is upside down. The laws of science can be broken. The earth is flat. And the great Neil Armstrong never made it to the moon. Welcome to the Weird Science Hall of Shame!

Hey, Chris. Some people still believe the world is flat.

Inconceivable!

The Flat Earth Society

Some people think that Christopher Columbus shocked the world in 1492 by proving that the Earth was round. In truth, at that time, the concept of a spherical Earth wasn't really all that shocking. The idea was first proposed by ancient Greek philosophers in the sixth century BCE and was generally accepted by the time Columbus set sail.

WORLD IS FLAT AND THAT'S THAT!

Today, we can fly around the globe. We can see satellite photos from space, showing Earth looking like a big blue marble. We know that our planet is not a perfect sphere, but instead, slightly flattened like a Nerf basketball that's been stepped on and hasn't quite gotten back into shape. (It's a little bit wider from side to side than it is from top to bottom. Scientists call it an oblate spheroid.)

In the face of all the evidence, there's a weird group who believes that the Earth isn't an oblate spheroid at all. Rejecting common sense and scientific proof, they insist that it's shaped like a big poker chip. They call themselves "The Flat Earth Society."

The Flat Earth Society has been around in various forms since 1849, when an Englishman named Samuel Birley Rowbotham published a sixteen-page pamphlet called "Earth Not a Globe." Rowbotham claimed that Earth was a big disk with the North Pole at the center. In Rowbotham's view, the continent of Antarctica was a big ring of ice at the disk's edge.

How deep is the poker chip? And what would happen if you pushed past the Antarctic ice ring? Would you fall off the edge? The whole theory falls apart if you give it a moment's thought, but that hasn't stopped it from finding believers for more than 150 years.

The current Flat Earth Society was officially formed in 1956. Its founder, Samuel Shenton, embraced Rowbotham's ideas and stubbornly refused to listen to reason. Presented with photographs of Earth from space, he dismissed them, saying, "It's easy to see how a photograph like that could fool the untrained eye."

Headlines from Flat Earth News

Australia Is Not Down Under!

Galileo Was a Liar

The Earth Is Not a Ball

Gravity Does Not Exist

Science Insults Your Intelligence

In the 1970s, the Flat Earth Society moved its headquarters to California and started publishing *Flat Earth News*. Sample headline: "World IS Flat and That's That." In recent times, it seemed like the Flat Earth Society had finally disbanded and gone away, but some bad ideas never die. The society was reformed in 2009, and its new website mentions that the group is using neurotransmitters to brainwash nonbelievers and makes a weird claim that had us scratching our heads in bewilderment: "Your dog has joined us."

It's nice to know that even a Flat Earther can have a sense of humor.

The Worlds Inside the World

If you stroll through Ludlow Park (also known as Symmes Park) in Hamilton, Ohio, you'll pass an odd-looking monument. From far away, it looks like a column holding up a big stone eyeball. But as you get closer, you'll see that the orb isn't an eyeball at all. It's a granite sculpture of Earth with a big hole at the top.

On the monument, there's an inscription that reads:

> CAPT. JOHN CLEVES SYMMES, AS A PHILOSOPHER, AND ORIGINATOR OF SYMMES THEORY OF CONCENTRIC SPHERES AND POLAR VOIDS; HE CONTENDED THAT THE EARTH IS HOLLOW AND HABITABLE WITHIN.

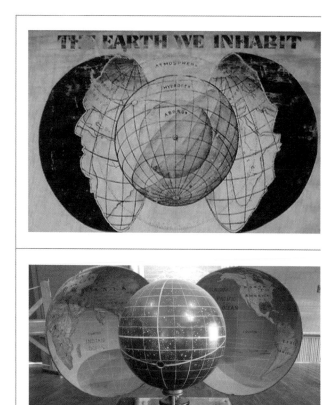

John Cleves Symmes, Jr. (1779–1829) was the father of the Hollow Earth theory, and this strange monument was constructed in the 1840s by his son, Americus Vespucci Symmes (who, like our country, was named after the famous Italian explorer, Amerigo Vespucci).

John Cleves Symmes wasn't a scientist. He was a captain in the army and, after leaving the military, ran a trading post in St. Louis. Still, he had a burning fascination for the natural sciences, and in 1818 he published his theory, addressing it, "To All the World."

Have you ever seen a nest of boxes—a box inside a box, inside a box, and so on? Symmes was convinced that the world was actually a nest of worlds—a world inside a world, which is inside a world, and so on. According to his theory, each inner world had a sun and each supported life, including subterranean plants, animals, and humans. Symmes insisted that the North and South Poles were actually entranceways, giant holes leading to the worlds inside our world. His fantasy was to lead an expedition into the hole at the North Pole.

In the leaflet announcing his theory, he wrote, "I ask 100 brave companions, well-equipped, to start from Siberia in the fall season with reindeer and sleighs on the frozen sea. I engage we find a warm rich land." Alas, Symmes's dream never came true. He never explored the Arctic and never found his paradise inside the hollow Earth; however, his ideas stirred the imagination of an Ohio newspaper editor named Jeremiah N. Reynolds. After Symmes died in 1829, Reynolds took up the cause, and ten years later, his efforts led to the first Antarctic expedition by the United States.

For four years, a team of Americans explored the frozen continent. They discovered new species of plants and animals and charted regions that had never been mapped. But they never found the polar portals that Symmes had predicted. Of course, this isn't surprising. The concept of polar holes leading to an underground fantasyland is science fiction, not science.

What's below Earth's crust? An extremely hot semisolid region called the mantle. And beneath the mantle is Earth's core. There are no frolicking inner-earth animals. No mysterious race of inner-earth humans. Yet, like the Flat Earth Society, the Hollow Earth theory still has a few believers, even today.

Many modern Hollow Earthers claim that there is an advanced civilization living inside our planet. And supposedly, these underground superbeings occasionally take trips to the outer world by journeying through the polar portals, often called Symmes's Holes. And how do you think they make these trips? They use flying saucers!

A monument to John Symmes, father of the hollow head—we mean hollow *Earth*—theory.

DO NOT DISTURB: ALIENS INSIDE.

The Face of Mars

In 1976, Viking Orbiter 1 was snapping pictures of the Cydonia region of Mars. NASA scientists were searching for a landing site for Viking Lander 2, and the orbiter's photos were going to help them make a decision. Suddenly, they received a photo that must have made them all smile. In the shot, among the hills, was a large object that resembled a human face.

Have you ever seen a face in a cloud? Seeing faces or other familiar images inside randomly shaped objects such as clouds is so common that it even has a name: *pareidolia*.

The "face" on Mars in the Viking Orbiter photo is an optical illusion, an obvious example of pareidolia. As you'd expect, NASA scientists didn't take it very seriously. In fact, no one paid it any attention until conspiracy theorist Richard Hoagland published his book *The Monuments of Mars*.

We see a big cloud. How about you?

Hoagland was convinced that the "face" was a huge stone carving, a gigantic Martian Mount Rushmore. He declared that Martians were also responsible for other amazing creations such as awesome pyramids and fantastic cities. According to Hoagland, NASA scientists had photographic evidence of these wonders, but they were withholding their findings because they were worried that news of an advanced civilization on Mars would cause fear and panic. Wow! All that from a blurry picture of a hill that looks like a face!

Technology has improved since the Viking missions, so later Martian probes have sent back more detailed pictures. In 1998, researchers received images of the Cydonia region from the Mars Global Surveyor. These pictures make it very clear that the Martian stone face was nothing but a craggy hill. Still, Hoagland was not convinced.

Finally, he backed down in 2007. Photos from the Mars Reconnaissance Orbiter were so sharp that even Hoagland had to admit that there was no "Face" on Mars. Now he's convinced that what he thought was a face was actually a collapsed Martian building.

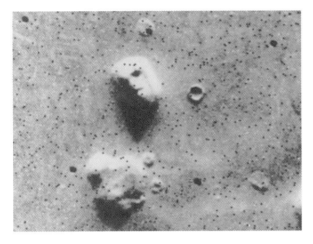

It sure looks like a face from here!

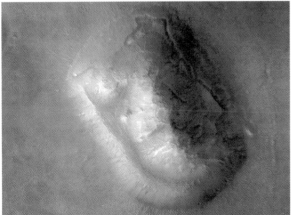

But up close . . . not so much.

Attack of the Martian Smileys!

If NASA scientists got a kick out of the "face" in the pictures from the Cydonia region, they must have had a belly laugh when they first saw pictures of Galle, a Martian crater, which was also photographed by Viking Orbiter 1. Looking like a humongous smiley face, Galle is now known as the "happy face crater." And it's not the only happy face on Mars. In 2008, another smiley appeared in photos from the Mars Reconnaissance Orbiter. Could these smiley faces be messages from Mars to Earth? Is an advanced Martian civilization trying to tell us, "Don't worry, be happy"? Nah! They are just curly shaped mountain ranges inside Martian impact craters. But they still make the angry, red planet seem a little more approachable.

Impossible Machines

Imagine a self-recharging electric scooter. It would come with a fully charged battery, and, as you putter around town, the scooter would recharge itself. The battery would never drain, so you could keep riding forever.

Sound nice? Well, you can't have one because it could never exist! Like all perpetual motion machines, it's impossible. Real science dictates that you can't get something for nothing! This is true in the supermarket and it's also true in *thermodynamics*, the branch of science that involves the conversion of energy from one form into another.

As you ride on your self-recharging scooter, energy would be lost due to friction. Every time you brake, you would need energy to make the bike slow down. And then it would take more energy to get you going again. Your self-recharging scooter could never produce more energy than is needed to keep it going, so eventually the scooter's battery would lose its charge, leaving you without power and forcing you to call for a ride home.

You can't get more energy out of a machine than you put in. In scientific terms: the laws of thermodynamics make perpetual motion machines impossible.

Over the years, many con artists have tried to make a buck by suckering the public with phony perpetual motion devices. These contraptions appear to run themselves, but there's always a hidden power source, keeping the machine in motion. One of the most persistent of all perpetual motion hoaxers was Charles Redheffer.

He first unveiled his invention in 1812 in a house on the banks of the Schuylkill River near Philadelphia, Pennsylvania. Redheffer wouldn't let onlookers get too close. But for the price of admission, he would let them gawk at his creation through a barred window.

Redheffer's perpetual motion machine marvel caused a sensation. Then, the con man got greedy and began to push his luck. Hoping to make a score, he applied for public funding so that he could build a larger machine. Big mistake!

On January 21, 1813, the government sent inspectors to take a look at Redheffer's invention. The team included a man named Nathan Sellers, and Sellers decided to bring along his son, Coleman. When young Coleman peeked through the little window, he saw a big machine powering a second smaller machine through interlocked gears. Amazingly, the larger machine seemed to be running by itself! Then Coleman noticed something odd. Studying the teeth of the gears, he realized that they were worn down on the wrong side. He realized that the big machine wasn't powering the little machine. It was the other way around! Coleman Sellers had discovered the hidden power source, and he revealed to his father that Redheffer's perpetual motion machine was a fake.

Exposed, Charles Redheffer skipped town and fled to New York, where he tried the same scam, except this time, his machine was far less convincing, and he was up against an even more brilliant opponent. Robert Fulton, the engineer who made steamboat travel in America a reality, checked out Redheffer's new perpetual motion scheme. Fulton noticed that the machine wasn't moving

The Zeroth Law

There are four laws of thermodynamics: the first law, the second law, the third law, and the Zeroth Law! Huh? Laws one, two, and three were developed first. The fourth law came last, but it was so important that it really should have been number one. After some head scratching, scientists decided to stick the last law up front and call it "The Zeroth Law of Thermodynamics." Fortunately, this numbering system hasn't caught on. Otherwise, you might win a race and be awarded zeroth place! And restaurants that don't take reservations might display signs saying, "Zeroth Come, Zeroth Served!"

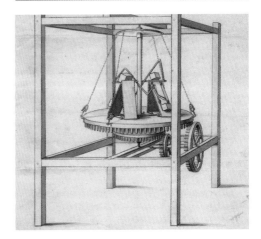

smoothly. It was wobbling. Prying loose a piece of the machine, the engineer found a string. He followed it to the next room, where he found an old man operating a hand crank while munching on a piece of bread. This was the wobbly, hidden source of power behind Redheffer's new invention.

Foiled again and frightened by the angry mob of New Yorkers who realized they'd been duped, Redheffer disappeared. We're not sure where he went or what happened to him. Maybe he learned his lesson and went clean. Or maybe, more likely, he changed his name and just kept moving, wandering from town to town, rolling his latest perpetual motion contraption behind him.

The Keely Machine

Is empty space completely empty? If not, what's inside the emptiness? These days, a physicist would probably give you a complicated answer, saying that space is a "partial vacuum." This means that space is mostly empty, except for a few stray particles and waves passing through.

In the late 1800s, physicists believed that space was filled with a mysterious substance called *ether*. No one knew much about ether, but they were convinced that it existed and that it was everywhere.

In 1872, a carpenter/mechanic and masterful showman, John Ernst Worrell Keely, announced that he'd discovered a way to extract incredible amounts of energy from the mysterious, all-present ether. To back up his claim, he tossed out a lot of pseudo-scientific mumbo jumbo, calling his amazing invention an "etheric generator" or a "hydro-pneumatic-pulsating-vacu-engine."

And if you like my Keely Machine, I've got a bridge in Brooklyn I'd like to sell you!

Starting the Keely Motor Company, he raised enough money to build his first Keely Machine. He claimed that, using a quart of water, his device would produce enough energy to fuel cross-country train trips. A gallon would be enough for international steamship voyages. "A bucket of water has enough of this vapor to produce a power sufficient to move the world out of its course," proclaimed Keely. Shocking as it may seem, people believed him.

In 1874, he gave a demonstration. He blew into a nozzle and poured in some water. Then, before an awestruck crowd in Philadelphia, his machine produced a tremendous amount of power. Later on, one witness described the event: "Great ropes were torn apart, iron bars broken in two or twisted out of shape, bullets discharged through twelve-inch planks, by a force which could not be determined."

Wealthy townspeople showered money on Keely. He produced more and more inventions, but he wouldn't explain how any of them worked. His exciting, new power source became less exciting as people gradually realized that his machines ran only if he was around to operate them. His investors demanded that he give up his secrets, but Keely refused and was put in prison for a short time.

The Keely Machine remained a mystery until Keely passed away in 1898. After his death, his laboratory was searched and all sorts of deceptions were uncovered. False ceilings and floors. Secret motors. Belt systems and hidden networks of pipes and electrical wires. And in the basement, investigators found a three-ton hollow sphere, most likely for compressed air. Keely had completely rigged the place so that he could stage his fantastic demonstrations. Some of Keely's faithful employees came up with farfetched explanations, hoping to defend their deceased boss. But it was obvious by then that John Ernst Worrell Keely was a fraud.

Keely's stock was as worthless as his inventions.

The Moon Hoax

For their tireless work, spreading nonsense and balderdash, the Weird Science Hall of Shame Zeroth Prize Award goes to (drumroll, please!): The Flat Earth Society! Remember them? Well, they're back!

When Apollo 11 landed on the moon in 1969, Flat Earthers didn't rejoice. This colossal event disproved their silly theory and so they decided that the moon landing never really took place. They insisted that the whole thing was a publicity stunt, a staged fake, shot like a Hollywood movie. According to them, Neil Armstrong's famous lunar walk was filmed on a soundstage in Borehamwood, England, and financed in part by Disney.

They proposed that the spectacle was directed by filmmaker Stanley Kubrick and written by Arthur C. Clarke, the team behind the science fiction movie *2001: A Space Odyssey*. Of course, no one was more surprised by these crazy claims than the people who were supposedly involved.

The members of the Flat Earth Society were the first to accuse NASA of fraud, but others have followed in their footsteps. Today, more than forty years after the Apollo 11 moon landing, there are still crackpots who believe it never happened. They study photos, hunting for possible fakery, and then they come out with arguments, which only show how little they know.

For example, "Moon Hoax" conspiracy theorists notice that, in photos, the lunar sky is empty and black. "Aha!" they cry. "Where are the stars? It's a fake! It's a fake!"

Did we really land on the moon, or was it all an elaborate hoax?

Astronauts Buzz Aldrin and Neil Armstrong training for their moon mission. Moon hoaxers believe NASA used similar sets to fake the moon landing.

Where are the stars? The answer is obvious to anyone with a beginner's knowledge of photography. When you take a picture, you can set your camera to photograph bright objects. Or you can adjust it to capture dim objects. But there's no setting that will let you do both. The Apollo 11 mission photos were taken in bright sunlight. If the camera had been set to capture the stars, then the moon would have looked washed out and featureless, and the photos would have been useless. No craters. No moon rocks. Just a glowing, white moon surface and a sky specked with stars.

Sadly, writers are still churning out books about the "Moon Hoax," and the gullible public is still buying them. Some new books even offer a new dumb spin on an already dumb conspiracy theory. Recently, in the book *Moon Landings: Did NASA Lie?* French author Philip Lheureux suggested that American astronauts landed on the moon secretly, and then, just to confuse everyone, NASA distributed phony pictures from a phony moon landing.

We're convinced . . . not!

Okay. Let's see if we can get this straight . . . NASA faked the moon landing in order to hide the fact that they landed on the moon? We can only hope that Lheureux's theory doesn't catch on. Besides being absurd, it's way too complicated!

The Philadelphia Experiment

In his 1955 book, *The Case for the UFO*, Morris K. Jessup imagined how flying saucers might be powered. He theorized about antigravity and about possible uses of the Unified Field Theory (or UFT), which Einstein worked on for years but was never able to finish.

Shortly afterward, Jessup claimed that he received a bizarre letter from a man named Carlos Miguel Allende. In this unusual note, Allende claimed that Einstein had solved the mysteries behind the UFT and that his discoveries had led to one of the weirdest experiments ever performed.

According to Allende, the Philadelphia Experiment was conducted in the Philadelphia Naval Yard in Pennsylvania during World War II. Supposedly, American scientists were researching a new technology using a destroyer called the *USS Eldridge*. Loaded with coils and generators, the *Eldridge* had been given a Dr. Frankenstein makeover. The idea was that the rigs would create strong electromagnetic fields and these fields would work together to make light bend around the ship. Effectively, the ship would become invisible.

The story goes that on July 22, 1943, the switches were flipped. The USS *Eldridge* vanished, leaving behind only a strange green fog. Fifteen minutes later, the ship reappeared. The experiment was a success with one not-so-minor glitch. The crew of the USS *Eldridge* felt extremely nauseous and disoriented.

In the letter, Allende proceeds to describe a follow-up experiment that took place a few months later. On October 28, 1943, the USS *Eldridge* disappeared once again, only to reappear 200 miles away in Norfolk, Virginia. Carlos Allende claims to have witnessed the trial from a nearby ship, the USS *Andrew Furuseth*.

Minutes later, the *Eldridge* was back in Philly. The ship was intact, but the crew unfortunately was not. Some crew members had gone insane. Others had been teleported to pieces. One man found himself on a different level of the ship from where he started. Weirder still, he was missing his hand, which was later found fused to the wall of the warship. And some members of the USS *Eldridge* never made it back at all. When the warship reappeared, they were simply missing. Afterward, the experiments were stopped, the evidence was concealed, and that was the end of Carlos Allende's chilling tale.

Who was Carlos Allende? Perhaps he was a local lunatic who suffered from science-fiction fever dreams. Or maybe he was a prankster who cooked up the Philadelphia Experiment as a practical joke. It's possible that the man didn't even exist, and the story was concocted by Jessup, who doesn't sound like the world's most reliable source, anyway.

Is it conceivable that Carlos Allende was telling the truth and that the Philadelphia Experiment actually happened? Let's put it this way, there are some who believe that the Philadelphia Experiment is fact, not fiction, and chances are these folks also believe that we never landed on the moon and that the world is hollow or flat. We at Weird Central like to keep our minds open, but . . . invisible warships? Teleportation? If the Philadelphia Experiment were even remotely plausible, we would have stuck it in the Freaky Physics chapter.

Now you see it . . .

Now you don't!

ACKNOWLEDGMENTS

Matt Lake:

I know that without John Lake, Chris Lake, and Arnold Toynbee I wouldn't be nearly as excited about history as I am. And without Julia, Nicole, Danny, Stephan, and Genea reminding me that I myself qualify as a historical artifact, I'd have less of a sense of humor about it. And without the Marks, I'd never have considered history as weird as it truly is. Thanks to all of you!

Randy Fairbanks:

I'm grateful to all of the aficionados of weirdness who helped on this book. Mark Moran and Mark Sceurman guided us with ever-watchful weird eyes. Matt Lake is a wonderful writer and a big fan of Benjamin Franklin and of all things bizarre—the perfect partner for a book on weird U.S. history. I'm glad I've had the opportunity to work with him. Thanks to our editor, Joe Rhatigan, for keeping the book tight, focused, and fun, and to the many unsung heroes behind this book: the contributors to Weird U.S. who have compiled a vast and indispensable archive of oddities. Also to my wife, Elizabeth Applegate, for her comments, encouragement, and funny dances. (Benjamin Franklin's toga-sporting, dancing ghost should take notes!) Special thanks to librarian Laura Follmer and to the kids at Goodnoe. My annual visits to your school help keep me writing. Stay weird!

INDEX

PHOTO CREDITS

All images © Weird NJ, Inc. or public domain except:

Page 5 bottom left and right, Library of Congress; 6 (both) Shutterstock; 7 bottom left Hkandy, top left Chris Huh, top right Mike Baird, middle right Stella Nutella at en.wikipedia; 8 left © Fernando Revilla, top right Roman Klementschitz, middle right, Shutterstock, bottom right © Geoff Shaw, bottom middle Quartl; 9 top right John Gould, center right © TwoWings, bottom right cliff1066™, middle (both) Shutterstock; 10 center left © iStock–Graeme Purdy, bottom left © Alexdi, right Piekfrosch; 11 left The.Rohit, right Shutterstock; 12 top left NOAA, bottom left © Edie Widder, right top and bottom, Wikipedia; 13 top right © C. Van Dover, bottom right Kils; 13 right NOAA, bottom NOAA; 14 left Sannse, right Shutterstock; 15 (all) Shutterstock; 16 middle left Habib M'henni, bottom left © Jon Sullivan, right Shutterstock; 17 top Shutterstock; 18 top © Nobu Tamura; 19 top USGS, bottom © Gerhard Elsner; 20 left Roger Manley, right Charmaine Ortega Getz; 21 top © City of Fruita, bottom Charmaine Ortega Getz; 23 top Joseph Citro, bottom © Ifremer/A. Fifis; 25 top right © Alamy.com, center courtesy Center for Disease Control and Prevention's Public Health Image Library, bottom courtesy Alexander Fleming Laboratory Museum (Imperial College Healthcare NHS Trust); 26 © Kmhkmn; 27 Library of Congress, pigeons and funny hat Shutterstock; 28 top Shutterstock, center © Michael J. Peterson, bottom Library of Congress; 29 top Library of Congress, bottom Shutterstock; 31 bottom Shutterstock; 32 top left and right, Library of Congress, bottom Shutterstock; 33 top Library of Congress; 34 Shutterstock; 35 Library of Congress; 36 all Shutterstock; 37 right Shutterstock; 38 Shutterstock; 40 top left Library of Congress; middle right Shutterstock, bottom right Joseph Wright; 41 Shutterstock; 42 bottom Mark Moran; 43 top PRA; 44 top Shutterstock; 45 all Shutterstock; 46 all Shutterstock except top right iStock; 47 left © Søren Wedel Nielsen, top right © UpstateNYer–Matt H. Wade, bottom right Shutterstock; 48 © www.pdphoto.org; 49 © Flagstaffotos; 50-51 © eepybird.com; 52 © Mark Moran; 55 left Ryan Doan/www.RyanDoan.com; 56 top right Ryan Doan, rest Shutterstock; 57 top NOAA, bottom Shutterstock; 58 bottom © Jabberocky; 60 Courtesy of Larry E. Arnold, ABLAZE!; 61 top Ryan Doan, center © Tahoenathan, bottom Greg Bishop; 62 top Shutterstock, bottom Wesley Treat; 63 top Mark Moran; 64 Shutterstock; 65 Library of Congress; 66 © J. Tautz and M. Kleinhenz, Beegroup Wurzburg; 67 top Library of Congress, bottom Shutterstock; 68 top Shutterstock, bottom left © iStock, bottom right © Alan D. Wilson www.naturespicsonline.com; 69 Shutterstock; 70-71 Shutterstock; 72 top Shutterstock, bottom © iStock; 73 Shutterstock; 74 NASA, illustrations Shutterstock; 75 NASA, 77 bottom left © iStock; 78 Shutterstock; 79 left center Library of Congress, right center and bottom Shutterstock; 80 top © iStock–cristimate, bottom NASA; 81 left and top right NASA, bottom right Shutterstock; 82 NASA; 83 top © courtesy of the Johnsville Centrifuge and Science Museum, bottom © iStock–Grafissimo; 84 middle © Chris Darling, bottom Shutterstock; 85 Shutterstock; 86 top © Jared C. Benedict, bottom left © Michael Malyszko used courtesy of the Museum of Science; bottom right (both) © Yoshiki Hase used courtesy of Museum of Science; 87 top and middle Shutterstock, bottom NASA; 88 NASA; 89 top and middle NASA; 90 right NASA, bottom left and right © Pretzelpaws, 91 top © Alain, middle NASA; 92 top © Karl Ragnar Gjertsen; 93 left Shutterstock; 94 top © iStock; 96 top right from the collection of Jack and Beverly Wilgus, bottom © Mysid; 97 Bundesarchiv, Bild 183-61478-0004/WeiB, Gunter/CC-BY-SA; 98 Shutterstock; 99 © ZenOptic; 101 Dr. Karlosi/Mark Moran; 102 NASA; 103 Shutterstock; 104 bottom © Mark Moran; 105 top James Willis; 106 top © Brian Waddellz, bottom NASA, 107 NASA; 108 Shutterstock; 110 Corbis; 112-113 NASA.

ABOUT THE AUTHORS

RANDY FAIRBANKS grew up in Stanhope, New Jersey, and has lived in Brooklyn, New York, since 1984. He studied math and physics at the University of Pennsylvania and filmmaking at NYU Graduate Film School. As a writer of children's stories, he appeared regularly as Uncle Randy on the weekly radio program *Greasy Kid Stuff* on WFMU. In 2007, he wrote *The Weird Club* and is currently collaborating with *Weird NJ* and Matt Lake on a series for kids. A lifelong fan of all things weird, Randy started a "Monster Club" in elementary school. He was the only member.

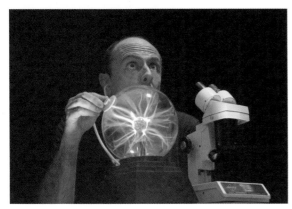

Like Frankenstein's monster, **MATT LAKE** is a tall, lumbering monster who speaks in grunts. Unlike Frankenstein's monster, Matt was assembled on a production line in the industrial city of Birmingham, England. Although he's a limited edition of one, Matt was machine-tooled with great precision to write and edit books on technology, history, and weirdness. He is the author of six *Weird* books and counting.

ABOUT WEIRD U.S.

Weird U.S. is Mark Moran and Mark Sceurman, otherwise known as "the Marks." The Marks have authored and/or published dozens of *Weird* books over the years and even starred in their own TV show. So, you may be wondering, how does the Weird U.S. staff decipher the fact from the fiction? How do they separate the science from the pseudoscience? They don't. They collect awesome stories and try, wherever possible, to corroborate these tales with historical data. Sometimes they are successful and manage to uncover a little-known tidbit of historical validity, and sometimes they don't. If they find that a local legend is patently untrue, do they refrain from publishing it? Absolutely not—especially if it's a great story! So, how will you know where to draw the line between fact and fantasy? That's for you to decide. Weird U.S. merely presents these stories in the most unadulterated form possible for you to ponder. One thing the folks at Weird U.S. will tell you though: None of the stories in this book are fiction—some might not be completely true, but none were made up solely for the purpose of entertainment.

SHOW US
YOUR WEIRD!

Do you know of a weird site found somewhere in the United States, or can you tell us about a strange experience you've had? If so, we'd like to hear about it! We believe that every town has at least one great tale to tell, and we're listening. It could be a cursed road, a haunted grocery store, an odd character, or a bizarre historic event. In most cases, these tales are told only in the towns in which they originated. But why keep them to yourself when you could share them with all of America? So come on and fill us in on all the weirdness that's lurking in your backyard!

You can e-mail us at: editor@weirdUS.com

Or write to us at:
Weird U.S.
P.O. Box 1346,
Bloomfield, NJ 07003
www.weirdus.com

Hey, you can also join our club for kids:
www.weirdclub.com